Interaction, Improvisation, and Interplay in Jazz

Interaction, Improvisation, and Interplay in Jazz

Robert Hodson
Hope College

Routledge
Taylor & Francis Group
New York   London

Routledge is an imprint of the
Taylor & Francis Group, an informa business

Routledge
Taylor & Francis Group
270 Madison Avenue
New York, NY 10016

Routledge
Taylor & Francis Group
2 Park Square
Milton Park, Abingdon
Oxon OX14 4RN

© 2007 by Taylor & Francis Group, LLC
Routledge is an imprint of Taylor & Francis Group, an Informa business

Printed in the United States of America on acid-free paper
10 9 8 7 6 5 4 3 2 1

International Standard Book Number-10: 0-415-97681-2 (Softcover) 0-415-97680-4 (Hardcover)
International Standard Book Number-13: 978-0-415-97681-7 (Softcover) 978-0-415-97680-0 (Hardcover)

Library of Congress Cataloging-in-Publication Data

Hodson, Robert, 1966-
    Interaction, improvisation, and interplay in jazz / Robert Hodson.
        p. cm.
        Includes bibliographical references (p.   ).
        ISBN 0-415-97680-4 -- ISBN 0-415-97681-2
        1. Jazz--History and criticism. 2. Improvisation (Music)--History. 3. Jazz--Social aspects. I. Title.

ML3506.H65 2007
781.65'1438--dc22   2006031341

Visit the Taylor & Francis Web site at
http://www.taylorandfrancis.com

and the Routledge Web site at
http://www.routledge-ny.com

Contents

Preface

This book arises from the confluence of my experiences as a performing musician and a music scholar. Originally a classical pianist, I also developed a strong interest in jazz, cultivated through listening to recordings, radio broadcasts, and attending live performances. I was particularly fascinated with and mystified by both the improvisational abilities of jazz musicians as well as the way that the members of small jazz ensembles coordinated their individual parts into cohesive, coherent performances.

As my increasing interest in jazz led me to a hands-on study of jazz improvisation and performance, I had the great fortune to encounter some excellent teachers as well as the priceless opportunity to perform weekly with some really fine, professional players. As I became more and more comfortable playing with these musicians, I began to notice interesting things going on around me during these performances. That is, I began to hear that the musicians were not just *coordinating* their individual improvised parts, but that there was an amazing amount of interaction going on between the players; the musicians were frequently responding to one another, engaging in musical conversations in which each musician's improvisation was, at times, affected and influenced by the other musicians' improvisations. At first, I was able to do little more than notice these interactions taking place around me, but as I gained experience, I found I was able to participate in these interactions. Through this experience, I gained a real appreciation for the dynamic, interactive processes that take place between jazz musicians, and realized that these interactions are an essential part of a jazz performance.

While pursuing a doctorate in music theory at the University of Wisconsin–Madison, I decided that I wanted to focus my research on jazz, and I began to survey the theoretical and analytical writings on jazz improvisation. As I read article after article, I noticed that the authors tended to focus on single improvised lines, rarely considering the possibility that the simultaneously improvised parts of the other members of the ensemble could have an effect on the solo line they were analyzing. In other words, they tended to ignore the dynamic, interactive processes that I found—and continue to find—to be so interesting in jazz performances. This book is my attempt to expand the scope of jazz theory and analysis beyond this narrow focus on a single improvised line. To this end, the first chapter develops a model of the improvisational process that includes player interaction as a fundamental principle, and all of my analyses will be built around the idea that jazz musicians do not improvise in isolation, and that a jazz performance is as much about what happens *between* musicians as it is about each musician's individual improvisation.

This book began as my doctoral dissertation, and I would particularly like to thank my adviser, Brian Hyer, for his guidance throughout that project. His tremendous generosity with his time and his careful reading and thoughtful comments on my many drafts had a profound effect on the final form of the dissertation and, as a result, this book. Brian provided me with an exemplary model of what it means to be a scholar, teacher, and mentor, and I hope to do for my students what he did for me.

I am currently on the faculty of Hope College in Holland, Michigan, and I would like to thank the college for supporting my work on this project. Provost James Boelkins and Dean for Arts and Humanities William Reynolds deserve special thanks for supporting this project through summer research grants and through assisting with publication expenses. Hope College is a great place to teach and work and I would like to thank my colleagues and my students in the music department for their questions, ideas, support, feedback, and positive energy.

I would like to acknowledge and express gratitude to those who taught me about jazz and how to play it. Lazaro Vega of WBLV Blue Lake Public Radio was my first jazz teacher; his nightly radio shows introduced me to jazz and taught me so much about this incredible music. Bassist Richard Davis also deserves special mention; his mentoring and friendship over the last dozen or so years has influenced me greatly. I'm also grateful to Ron Newman, Peter Dominguez, Marcus Belgrave, Eddie Russ, Andrew Speight, and Mtafiti Imara for their roles in my jazz education and performing experience.

Finally, I would like to thank my wife, Carrie, for her boundless love and support. To her, and to our children, Isabel and Simon, I dedicate this book with love and affection.

1

Jazz Improvisation
Theory, Analysis, Context, and Process

Most technical writings on jazz focus on improvised lines and their underlying harmonic progressions. These writings often overlook the basic fact that when one listens to jazz, one almost never hears a single improvised line, but rather a texture, a musical fabric woven by several musicians in real time. While it is often pragmatic to single out an individual solo line (I will be doing the same), it is important at all times to remember that an improvised solo is but one thread in that fabric, and it is a thread supported by, responded to, and responsive of the parts being played by the other musicians in the group. This book will explore the process of player interaction in jazz, and the role this interaction plays in generating improvised music.

I'd like to begin by examining a recorded excerpt from an improvisation by saxophonist Cannonball Adderley. To some extent, recordings in jazz take the place—and assume the same textual authority—of scores in European music, and I will rely on them throughout this work. Furthermore, I will make extensive use of transcriptions in my analyses, and while the authority of transcription has been widely critiqued in ethnomusicological circles,[1] I intend to circumvent that issue by viewing transcriptions as heuristics in my discussions of recorded performances. In other words, my transcriptions are meant to serve as visual aids to the recordings and to my commentaries on them. I do not assume that they capture all aspects of a recorded performance, and I will be routinely taking information into account that is not available in the transcription. I regard them as representations of performances rather than pieces, and at times those representations will be approximate—some of the music I will be dealing with is extremely complicated by the standards of any music notational tradition. It is important to remember that in jazz, a score (whether a "lead sheet," arrangement, or transcription) occupies no privileged ontological position, a notion that I take as an article of faith; my use of them is entirely pragmatic.

The excerpt, transcribed in figure 1.1, comes from the end of Adderley's first improvised chorus on the jazz standard "Groovin' High."[2] As a starting point, the analysis will first examine Adderley's improvised line by itself, before demonstrating that an examination of the musical context within which the improvisation took place can generate further insight. The analysis will introduce and briefly address a number of musical and analytical issues to be dealt with at length in later chapters.

Rests in mm. 27 and 28 suggest a preliminary parsing of the improvisation into three large gestures, which are bracketed in figure 1.1 and labeled A, B, and C. Each gesture is of a different length: A is nine beats long, beginning in m. 25 and extending through the downbeat of m. 27; B is approximately four beats long, beginning with a pick-up to beat 3 of m. 27 and extending to m. 28, beat 2; and C, the longest of the three, extends approximately fourteen beats from a pick-up to beat 4 of m. 28 through the downbeat of m. 32.

At first glance, comparing the scalar sixteenth-note improvised lines of gestures A and B with the somewhat less-scalar eighth-note line of gesture C suggests that this excerpt is made up of two quite different kinds of music. The following analysis supports that preliminary intuition, first describing the differences between gestures A–B and gesture C, and then suggesting possible reasons for these differences.

Besides sharing a preponderance of sixteenth notes, gestures A and B have many other similarities. As noted earlier, they are primarily scalar—that is, they are almost exclusively composed of stepwise motion—and both gestures are highly chromatic. A and B are also similar in another, less obvious, way in that both the contour and the melodic pitches of the improvised lines relate to the underlying harmony. Comparing gestures A and B with the underlying harmony reveals some consistent harmonic processes. Figure 1.2 presents a "harmonic analysis" of these melodic gestures. The upper staff adds analytical beams to the transcription, the middle staff gives a crude, "close position" realization of the chord symbols; these chords are

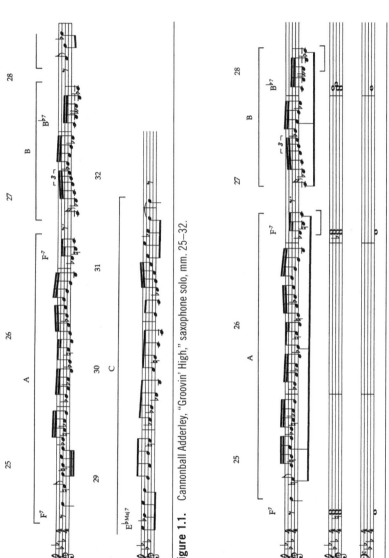

Figure 1.1. Cannonball Adderley, "Groovin' High," saxophone solo, mm. 25–32.

Figure 1.2. Cannonball Adderley, "Groovin' High," saxophone solo, mm. 25–28.

presented over a simple realization of the chord progression's root movement on the lower staff. The chord symbols in this figure are standard in jazz performance practice, and are interpreted as follows: The superscript $^{-7}$ denotes a minor seventh chord, constructed from a minor triad and minor 7th; the symbol C^{-7} would therefore designate the chord containing the pitches C, E♭, G, and B♭. The plain superscript ^{7} denotes a "dominant" seventh chord, made up of a major triad and minor 7th; C^{7} would therefore be C–E–G–B♭. The superscript ^{Maj7} designates a major seventh chord, containing a major triad and major 7th; C^{Maj7} would thus be spelled C–E–G–B. Finally, these chords may contain additional alterations: $C^{-7(♭5)}$, for instance, would designate a C minor seventh chord with a flatted-5th, or C–E♭–G♭–B♭.

As the added beams in figure 1.2 demonstrate, the contour of the improvised line emphasizes harmonically significant pitches: after the initial B♭ moves down to A (the 3rd of F^{7}), the line ascends to its high point, C (the 5th), before descending chromatically to E♭ (the 7th). E♭ is even more strongly emphasized than the previous harmonic pitches A and C for several reasons: (1) as an eighth note, E♭ receives an agogic accent after the long string of sixteenths; (2) it also receives a metric accent as a result of its falling *on* the beat; and (3) it is approached by double chromatic neighbors—F♭ above and D♮ below. As the two brackets below the upper staff in figure 1.2 point out, Adderley employs this double chromatic neighbor figure motivically, transposing it just after the downbeat of m. 27 to embellish C (the 5th of F^{7}) at the end of the first gesture and again in m. 28 to embellish A♭ (the 7th of $B♭^{7}$) at the end of gesture B. These double neighbors, when combined with the following rests, bring about a sense of melodic closure, and help define the endings of these gestures. Gesture B not only ends with the same closing motive as gesture A, but also like A emphasizes harmonically significant pitches through its contour, beginning on A♭ (the 3rd of F^{-7}), ascending to an embellished F (the root of F^{-7}), passing through B♭ (the root of $B♭^{7}$), before finally descending to A♭ (the 7th of $B♭^{7}$).

Another similarity between gestures A and B worth noting is the rhythmic placement of these harmonically significant pitches. Without exception, all of these pitches occur in relatively weak rhythmic positions—either off the beat (as in the first two beamed pitches of

Figure 1.3. E♭ minor pentatonic scale.

Figure 1.4. Cannonball Adderley, "Groovin' High," saxophone solo, mm. 29–32.

each gesture) or, if on the beat, on the metrically weak second beat of the measure (as in the third beamed pitch of each gesture). This rhythmic displacement of harmonic pitches keeps the music off balance and pushes it forward, making the improvised melody seem as if it floats over the meter, rather than being constrained by it.

Gesture C contrasts markedly with gestures A and B. Immediately noticeable is the change from sixteenth to eighth notes. Also noticeable is the fact that the melody of gesture C is not as consistently stepwise as the melodies in A and B, but contains a greater variety of melodic intervals. This contrast is, in part, a result of the melodic resources used in each gesture: A and B are constructed from a combination of chromatic and diatonic scales that Adderley uses to fill in gaps between chord tones, while C is constructed primarily from an E♭ minor pentatonic scale, written out in figure 1.3. The minor pentatonic scale is frequently used by improvisers to give the music a "bluesy" or "funky" feel. This bluesy feel derives from the use of "blue" notes—primarily the flatted 3rd G♭ and 7th D♭, which in figure 1.4 clash colorfully with the G♮ and D♮ of the underlying E♭$^{\text{Maj7}}$.

Figure 1.4 shows not only the clashes that result from playing the E♭ minor pentatonic scale over E♭$^{\text{Maj7}}$, but also that gesture C differs from A and B in the rhythmic placement of its harmonic pitches. Whereas in figure 1.2 we saw that chromatic neighbors displaced harmonic pitches to relatively weak rhythmic positions throughout A and B, harmonic pitches in C regularly occur *on* the beat, frequently right on the *first* beat of the measure. This has the effect of "rooting" the melody to the

	Gestures A-B	Gesture C
Rhythmic values:	faster (sixteenths)	slower (eighths)
Rhythmic subdivision:	more even (straight)	less even (swing)
Meter:	de-emphasized	emphasized
Melody:	more scalar	less scalar
Melodic resources:	chromatic scale, modes	minor pentatonic scale
Pitch:	more accurate/	less accurate/
	less inflected	more inflected
Harmonic pitch placement:	more syncopated	less syncopated

Figure 1.5. Comparison of gestures A–B and gesture C.

beat, binding it to the meter, in contrast to the way the melody breaks free and hovers above the meter in gestures A and B.

In addition to the differences discussed so far, two more very subtle differences exist between gestures A-B and gesture C. These differences—which are difficult if not impossible to capture in standard musical notation—have to do with subtle manipulations of pitch and rhythm. In gesture C, pitches tend to be *inflected*—that is, they may go in and out of tune, or rather "slid up" to, "squeezed," or "smeared," to use common jazz lingo—in contrast to the precise, in-tune pitches of gestures A and B. Subdivisions of the beat in A and B are also more precise than that of C: in A and B, the melody divides the beat into four *very* even sixteenths, while in C, the beat is divided into two *uneven* notes, the first longer and the second shorter. In jazz slang, the sixteenths in gestures A and B are played "straight," while Adderley "swings" the eighths in C. The long/short pattern of the swing eighths further emphasizes the beat in gesture C, increasing the difference in "feel" between it and gestures A and B.

Figure 1.5 summarizes some of the crucial differences between gestures A–B and gesture C. What intuition suggested *before* the analysis is confirmed by the analysis: the improvised line of gesture C is a different *kind* of music than that of gestures A and B—it is constructed differently and operates under different principles. The characteristics of these two different kinds of music correspond to two different styles of jazz: the first style, used in gestures A and B, is heard as *bebop,* and the second style, that used in gesture C, is heard as *blues.* So, between gestures B and C, Adderley shifts musical gears, switching from one style to another.

Up to this point, the analysis merely describes *how* Adderley switches from one style to another. A more interesting question is

"*Why* does Adderley make the switch from bebop to blues?" A number of explanations might be offered. Maybe after the long string of sixteenths, Adderley sensed a need for variety. Maybe he wanted to increase the energy level at the end of the chorus, but had reached his upper limit with the sixteenth-note lines, and switched to the more "vocal" blues style to make a stronger rhetorical statement. Maybe there isn't a strictly musical reason, and the change was just the result of a whim. Any of these reasons could be argued, but an additional possibility that can be even more strongly argued appears upon examination of the musical context within which the line was improvised.

Adderley's improvisation takes place in the context of a small-group jazz performance. A small jazz group usually consists of a rhythm section (piano, bass, and drums) and one or more "front-line" instruments, usually saxophone, trumpet, or trombone. The ensemble on this recording features a rhythm section made up of Wynton Kelly, piano, Percy Heath, bass, and Art Blakey, drums, and these are the musicians who accompany Adderley's improvisation. Even though standard jazz performance practice assigns certain musical roles to each member of the rhythm section (the drummer plays rhythmic patterns, the bassist "walks" a quarter-note line that defines the harmonic progression, and the pianist plays syncopated chords, or "comps"), the way that the members choose to fulfill these roles is flexible and often spontaneously negotiated in performance (rhythm section roles are discussed in more detail later in this chapter). In other words, *all of the members of the ensemble are improvising simultaneously;* the improvised saxophone melody is supported by the rhythm section's equally improvised accompaniment.

Examining Wynton Kelly's comping suggests another possible explanation for Adderley's change in style between gestures B and C. Through A and B, Kelly's comping is understated and fairly standard—he plays light, syncopated chords, providing rhythmic and harmonic support to Adderley's solo. However, in the break between Adderley's gestures B and C, he inserts a stronger, louder, fuller chord—in effect, he dramatically *punctuates* Adderley's improvisation. This particular chord "voicing," notated in figure 1.6, is remarkably colorful. Besides containing the root B♭, 3rd D, 7th A♭, and 13th G of B♭7, it also contains the blue notes D♭ and G♭ that clash with these chord members.

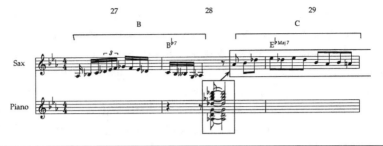

Figure 1.6.   "Groovin' High," mm. 27–29.

The most common blue notes arise from the clash between major and minor 3rds. In this voicing, both D, the major 3rd of the B♭⁷ chord, and G, the third scale-degree in E♭ major, are played at the same time as their blue notes D♭ and G♭. With this dramatically placed, very bluesy chord voicing, Kelly asserts or "signifies" the blues.[3]

Kelly's strong, bluesy voicing of this chord seems to have a galvanizing effect on the performance. It's almost as if Adderley hears this chord, draws upon the knowledge of jazz styles he shares with Wynton Kelly, realizes that this harmonic configuration signifies the blues style, and responds to Kelly's assertion by continuing his improvisation in a blues idiom. This type of interaction might be compared to a conversation: Kelly suggests a "topic" (the blues style), Adderley "responds" by elaborating on the topic. For the conversational metaphor to hold, though, the communication between the players would of course have to flow in both directions; further reflection on this performance shows this to be the case.

Figure 1.7 continues the transcription into the beginning of the next chorus. Adderley begins this chorus by introducing a two-note motive—the tonic E♭ preceded by its leading tone D—which he repeats and

Figure 1.7.   "Groovin' High," mm. 33–35.

develops over the next few measures. Kelly hears this simple, yet strong, motivic idea and responds immediately, adopting the D–E♭ neighbor figure as the uppermost notes in his chord voicing. Over the next few measures, both Adderley's and Kelly's improvisations are controlled by this motive.

This analysis shows that communication and interaction between players in small-group jazz can and frequently does affect an individual musician's improvisation. Indeed, the ability to listen and respond to one's bandmates is highly valued among jazz musicians. This dynamic interaction between simultaneously improvising musicians is the subject of this book: while most analyses of jazz improvisation tend to focus on the structure of an individual musician's improvised line, my analyses will consider not only these individual improvisations, but also the structure of interaction *between* the musicians in an ensemble, and will explore the ways this interaction can influence each individual musician's improvisation.

On the Nature and Analysis of Jazz Improvisation and Performance

The analysis of jazz improvisation presents some difficulties. First, since most of a jazz performance is improvised, there is no score to examine; typically, an analyst will want to create a transcription to aid the discussion of a recorded performance. Besides this practical difficulty, analyzing improvisation raises a number of larger issues, alluded to above, including the following: Is a transcribed improvisation comparable to a composed score? Are existing analytical models, which were devised for the analysis of composed scores, appropriate for the examination of an improvised solo? What should be our goal in analyzing improvised music? In other words, what is the nature of jazz improvisation and performance?

With regard to the issue of whether a transcribed improvisation is comparable to a composed score and can be analyzed as such, a number of authors express different viewpoints. These viewpoints can be boiled down to the question of whether an improvisation is viewed as a product or a process. If the improvisation is viewed as a product—comparable, that is, to a composed score—then existing analytical models can be used. Steve Larson and Steven Block have both taken this approach. In "Schenkerian Analysis of Modern Jazz," Larson applies Schenkerian analysis to improvisations by Thelonious Monk, Bill Evans, and Oscar Peterson, uncovering large-scale linear continuities.[4] This approach works especially well when considering improvisations by Bill Evans, who has acknowledged in interviews a tendency to conceive of his improvisations in terms of long-range voice-leading.[5] Block's "Pitch Class Transformation in Free Jazz," on the other hand, uses the tools and techniques of set theory to uncover harmonic and melodic organization in improvisations of Ornette Coleman, John Coltrane, Cecil Taylor, and others.[6] Figure 1.8 reproduces Block's analysis of the opening of Coltrane's improvised solo on the title track of the recording *Ascension*.[7] Block does an excellent job of demonstrating how Coltrane's improvised solo can be heard in terms of manipulations and transformations of pitch-class sets. Specifically, he argues that Coltrane generates the first half of this excerpt (mm. 1–16) by using two similar trichords (3-2 and 3-3), while in the second half (mm. 17–24), he switches to stringing together various transpositions of trichord 3-7.[8] Furthermore, he says that the composite tetrachord created by combining the specific 3-2 and 3-3 trichords of the first half results in a tetrachord (4-3) that can be transformed into the tetrachord (4-26) created by combining the first two 3-7 trichords of the second half.

Although the arithmetical rigor of Block's analysis is impressive, by focusing strictly on quantitative set-theoretical issues he tends to ignore more qualitative musical issues. Besides contrasting the pitch-class content of the first and second halves of the improvisation, one could also compare their difference in musical "character": in the first half, Coltrane seems to be thinking rhythmically, repeatedly grouping eighth notes in threes, creating a cross-rhythm with the clearly stated 4/4 meter provided by the rhythm section. In the second half, when he switches to basing his improvisation on the 3-7 trichord, his improvisation also changes in character, featuring longer, arcing melodic gestures. A more holistic analysis might consider the relationship between the change in the quantitative materials (the pitch-class sets) and this qualitative change in character. Furthermore, considering the rhythm section's accompaniment might lend additional insight into how Coltrane generates his improvisation. For example,

Figure 1.8. Steven Block's analysis from "Pitch Class Transformation in Free Jazz."

toward the end of the first half of the excerpt, pianist McCoy Tyner begins repeating the whole-step tone cluster A♭–B♭; it is Coltrane's subsequent emphasis on these same pitches that facilitates the change to trichord 3-7 beginning in m. 17.[9]

Other writers take a different approach, viewing improvisation as something intrinsically different from composed music, and focus their analyses on the improvisational process. In "A New Look at Improvisation," Ed Sarath describes the main difference between composition and improvisation as one of temporality:

> [In composition,] the composer generates the material in one time frame and encodes them in a work in another. . . . The composer enters the 'timescape' of a work, and yet may also step back to isolate, reflect on, and possibly revise any given moment. . . . By 'improvisation,' I mean the spontaneous creation and performance of musical materials in a real-time format, where the reworking of ideas is not possible.[10]

He argues that because of the fundamental difference in temporal orientation of composition and improvisation, analytical models created for the examination of composed music are not as useful for the analysis of improvisation. Perhaps the author to deal most extensively with the product/process distinction is Charles Keil. In "Motion and Feeling through Music," first published in 1966, Keil argues for an analytical approach to jazz performance that focuses on musical *process*.[11] This article was written in response to Leonard Meyer's *Emotion and Meaning in Music*,[12] which, according to Keil, approaches music entirely in terms of syntax:

> [Meyer] develops his thesis by first examining the form of music, a succession of tones, and then relating this form via psychological principles to meaning and expression. This procedure . . . implies not only a one-to-one relationship between syntactic form and expression but a weighting in favor of the former factor to the detriment of the latter. This tight equation of form and expression that for Meyer equals "embodied meaning" yields excellent results when applied to the generally through-composed and harmonically oriented styles of our own Western tradition. . . . When, however, this equation and the corresponding evaluative criteria are applied to non-Western styles . . . we often find that something is missing.[13]

	Embodied Meaning	Engendered Feeling
1. Mode of Construction	composed	improvised
2. Mode of Presentation	repeated performance	single performance
3. Mode of Understanding	syntactic	processual
4. Mode of Response	mental	motor
5. Guiding Principles	architectonic (retentive)	"vital drive" (cumulative)
6. Technical Emphases	harmony/melody/ embellishment (vertical)	groove/meter/ rhythm (horizontal)
7. Basic Unit	"sound term" (phrase)	gesture (phrasing)
8. Communication Analogues	linguistic	paralinguistic (kinesics, proxemics, etc.)
9. Gratifications	deferred	immediate
10. Relevant Criteria	coherence	spontaneity

Figure 1.9. Keil's Table of Contrasts.

What Keil finds missing in Meyer's syntactically focused notion of "embodied meaning" is any substantive consideration of musical process, and in response, Keil proposes an alternative set of musical characteristics that contribute to what he calls "engendered feeling." He compares several differences between these two aspects of musical experience in the table of contrasts reproduced in figure 1.9 (338).

Keil uses this list to contrast specific characteristics of European music and what he calls an "African or African-derived music" such as jazz. He says that European music, being composed, lends itself to repeated performances; jazz, on the other hand, being improvised, cannot be repeated exactly, and therefore can exist only as a single performance. In items 3 and 4 on his list, he seems to reify a mind/body dualism, saying that European music creates a mental response through syntactical organization, while jazz creates a more physical, motor response through musical process. He clarifies this in items 5 and 6, saying that "in composed music the structure or architecture is obviously of great importance; broadly speaking, melody rests upon harmony and embellishment upon melody" (344). Jazz, in contrast, places primary importance on the "vital drive," or "groove" that the musicians create (Keil's explanation of the ways that musicians create "vital drive" and "groove" will be examined more closely later in this chapter). In items 7 and 8, he again develops his mind/body dualism, saying that European music—with its emphasis on the syntactical content of a phrase—lends itself to linguistic analogy, while jazz—which places less emphasis on the *content* of a phrase and more emphasis on the gesture and sense of movement it creates—is better described in terms of kinesthetics. Finally, in items 9 and 10, he contrasts the ultimate goals of both kinds of music, saying that in European music "resolutions must be anticipated and patiently awaited, gratifications must be deferred" (346), and that the ultimate arrival of these resolutions gives a composition a sense of coherence. On the other hand, he says that since jazz's guiding principle of "vital drive" is present continuously throughout a performance, the gratification is not deferred, but immediate, that this lack of deferred gratification relaxes the need for any long-range sense of closure, and that, therefore, jazz performers place more emphasis on the perceived spontaneity of a given gesture rather than on its coherence to the performance as a whole.

Keil acknowledges that whereas most music involves aspects of both syntactical "embodied meaning" and processual "engendered feeling," certain kinds of music lean one way or the other; specifically, he says that the music of the Western tradition tends toward embodying meaning, while the primary goal of an "African-derived" style such as jazz is to engender feeling. Therefore, he argues, an analysis that focuses exclusively on structural, syntactical aspects of a jazz performance overlooks the most important aspects of the performance: the way that it engenders feeling through subsyntactical musical processes. I feel that in criticizing Meyer's focus on musical syntax, Keil perhaps swings too far in the other direction, narrowly focusing on—and overemphasizing almost to the point of fetishizing—subsyntactical processes, and as a result ignores the fact that, while subsyntactical aspects are an important part of a jazz performance, jazz musicians also use syntactical means such as goal-oriented harmonic progressions and melodies, motivic development, and recurring phrase structures to create an "architectonic" sense of deferred gratification and coherence.

Before defining my perspective on this issue, I'd like to briefly discuss Jean-Jacques Nattiez's ideas regarding the nature of the musical object as presented in *Music and Discourse: Toward a Semiology of Music*.[14] Nattiez says that a musical work is "three dimensional"—it consists not only of (1) a score, which he calls the "trace," but also (2) the compositional processes that led to its creation, as well as (3) the perceptual/cognitive responses of the listener. Figure 1.10 reproduces Nattiez's diagram of these three music-ontological dimensions. In this

Figure 1.10. Nattiez's three dimensions of a musical work.

Figure 1.11. Nattiez's model modified to describe jazz.

diagram the Poietic (or compositional) process produces the "trace," or score, which is realized by a performer or group of performers. The resulting performance is then heard by the listener, who perceives and cognizes the performance through Esthesic processes. Nattiez's ideas provide a nice compromise in the argument over whether jazz improvisation should be viewed as a product or a process. According to Nattiez, music is *both* product *and* process; a musical analysis should not only examine the trace (or product), but also consider the processes that led to its creation as well as a listener's perceptual and cognitive response.

Figure 1.11 modifies Nattiez's diagram to more accurately describe the "three dimensions" of a *jazz* performance. Since jazz is substantially improvised in performance, the poietic process and the performance occur at the same time in the same person—in other words, the musician composes and performs simultaneously without the intermediate step of writing the improvisation down. As a result, the only trace is the sound produced by the performer, which is received by the listener, initiating the esthesic process of perception and cognition.

In order to adequately describe the perspective of the jazz musician, the diagram needs one further modification, shown in figure 1.12. In small-group jazz, all of the musicians are improvising simultaneously. The additional arrow in this example accounts for the fact that besides being a composer and performer each musician in the group is also a *listener*—that is, they are hearing the traces produced by the other musicians, and deciding whether or not they will alter their improvisations based on what they hear. Thus, this diagram describes a (not quite) closed loop that is occurring around each musician: the

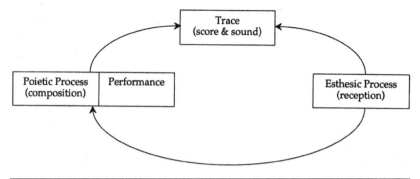

Figure 1.12.   Nattiez's model modified to describe improviser's perspective.

jazz musician decides what to improvise, plays it, hears the other musicians improvising, at which point the process starts all over again, in almost immediate succession. In the next section, "Musical Roles and Behaviors," I will consider specific constraints that each member of a small jazz ensemble has over the ways that they combine poietic and esthesic processes in the generation of their improvised parts.

To demonstrate the insights we can gain through adapting Nattiez's model to describe a jazz performance, I would like to briefly examine and critique a published analysis of Miles Davis's improvised solo on the tune "So What." The performance is from the 1959 album *Kind of Blue*,[15] and the analysis is from William Thomson's 1998 *College Music Symposium* article entitled "On Miles and the Modes."[16] Thomson analyzes Davis's solo in order to critique the concept of "modal jazz," a term often used to describe jazz performances in which long sections of music are based on a "mode" rather than a series of chords that may move through several different key centers (modal jazz will be discussed more thoroughly in chapter 4). The tune "So What" is often considered paradigmatic of modal jazz; as shown in figure 1.13, it is a thirty-two-bar AABA form, in which the A sections are based on the D dorian mode, whereas the B section is based on E♭ dorian.

Thomson says that while the concept of modal jazz may have influenced the creation of the recorded performance of "So What,"

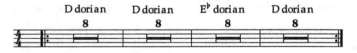

Figure 1.13.   "So What," formal sketch.

Figure 1.14.   "So What," Miles Davis's solo, mm. 1–16.

whether a listener can perceive this performance as "modal" is another matter. He begins by examining Davis's first improvised chorus, transcribed in figure 1.14. He says that in this chorus, Davis begins "with the best of dorian intentions" by emphasizing D and A in the first sixteen measures of his improvisation, and that by doing this he helps to project the "aura" of D dorian (21).

The crux of Thomson's argument appears when he considers the first eight measures of Davis's second improvised chorus, transcribed in figure 1.15. Here, he says, Davis's strong emphasis on the pitches C, E, and G destroys the sense of D as a "prevailing nucleus," and he describes this section as sounding more like "unrequited" C major than D dorian (25). He argues that not only does Davis's emphasis on the C major triad weaken the overall sense of D-ness, but also this emphasis on C major is so strong that a listener *cannot* perceive the melody at this point as being in D dorian. He then goes on to make the broader argument that the concept of modal jazz, although perhaps useful as a compositional tool, doesn't necessarily reflect the way a listener hears

Figure 1.15.   "So What," Miles Davis's solo, mm. 32–41.

Figure 1.16. "So What," Miles Davis's solo, mm. 1–8.

the music, and therefore is of limited usefulness when analyzing or theorizing a listener's perception of this kind of performance.

To rephrase Thomson's argument in terms of Nattiez's model, there is a putative disparity between the performers' poietic and the listener's esthesic processes; that is, the poietic process of basing an improvisation on a specific mode results in a sonic trace that doesn't necessarily convey that process to the listener. A crucial point that Thomson's analysis and argument overlooks is that the transcription of Davis's individual improvised melody is not an objectively "accurate" representation of the sonic trace heard by the listener. Rather, the listener hears Davis's solo within the musical context provided by the rhythm section, which consists of pianist Bill Evans, bassist Paul Chambers, and drummer Jimmy Cobb. Examining a transcription of all four musicians' improvised parts can give a better idea of this sonic context. In figure 1.16, which transcribes the first eight measures of Davis's solo, we can see how each of their parts relates to the prevailing

Figure 1.17. "So What," Miles Davis's solo, mm. 32–41.

D dorian mode: Paul Chamber's bass line walks up and down the mode with occasional chromatic passing notes, while Bill Evans's piano voicings colorfully combine 4ths and 3rds, planing pandiatonically through the pitches of the D dorian mode. In this excerpt, all of the musicians are working within D dorian, and their improvised parts all help to convey that to the listener.

If we turn our attention to a full transcription of the beginning of Davis's second chorus, shown in figure 1.17, we see how Thomson's argument begins to falter. As Davis begins to wander away from D and A, basing his improvised melody on the pitches C, E, and G, the other members of the rhythm section counter this by ever more strongly emphasizing D: Paul Chambers plays a bass ostinato made up of pitches D, F, and A, and Bill Evans's piano voicings more explicitly define D dorian, being made up of a D minor triad with the addition of an alternation between B♮ and C. Again, Thomson insists that

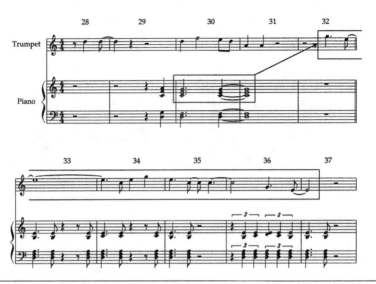

Figure 1.18. "So What," Miles Davis's solo, mm. 28–37.

because Davis's improvised line centers on C, E, and G, it *cannot* be perceived as being a D dorian melody. On the contrary, I think that given the strong emphasis on D by the piano and bass, Davis's line cannot be heard as anything *but* a melody in D dorian—a somewhat dissonant, colorful melody to be sure—but nevertheless a melody consisting of the 7th, 9th, and 11th of a tertian stacking of the pitches of the D dorian mode, rather than the root, 3rd, and 5th of C major.

Whereas we have been focusing on the performer's poietic processes relative to a (nonperforming) listener's esthesic processes, refocusing this analysis toward the perspective of the musicians taking part in the performance also yields interesting results. As we saw in the modification of Nattiez's diagram to reflect the improvisational process in figure 1.12, improvising musicians engage in a dynamic, interactive process of deciding what to play, playing it, hearing what the other musicians are playing, and adapting what they play to take into account the other musicians' improvisations. Such give-and-take between musicians seems to take place in this performance of "So What." In figure 1.18, which transcribes the measures leading up to Davis's second chorus—that is, the chorus in which he bases his improvisation on the pitches C, E, and G—we can see a series of musical events in which the musicians seem to respond to one another. Three measures before the beginning of this second chorus, Bill Evans plays a chord voicing containing C, E, and G as its top three pitches. Since this is the first time in the performance that he plays this voicing, it's possible that Davis's subsequent emphasis on these three pitches is a response to Evans. In fact, beginning at this point, we can theorize an interesting chain of interactions: Evans plays a voicing emphasizing C, E, and G, which Davis registers, as it were, improvising a melody containing these pitches, which in turn affects the way Evans and Chambers improvise their accompaniment to this melody: they strongly emphasize D dorian in order to balance out this melody's tonal ambiguity.

In adapting Nattiez's model to describe the perspective of a jazz musician, I've laid the groundwork for my views on the process/product question and set up the analytical perspective that will be used throughout this work: I will analyze the product of an improvisation (in the form of a transcription) in order to deduce processes that contributed to its generation. The analyses will attempt to bridge the gap and relax the tension between Keil's "embodied meaning" and "engendered feeling"; that is, they will explore the ways that improvising jazz musicians balance the constraining factors of the structural, syntactical aspects of the composition they are performing with the dynamic, interactive processes that take place between the members of the ensemble.

Since the analyses will focus on improvisational process, the music will be examined as an "in-time" phenomenon—musical events are considered in the order in which they occur. The analyses will, in effect, slow down the performance process and consider the effects of musical events as they occur, especially focusing on the transfer of ideas between players in real time. This kind of approach is similar to that of certain strains of phenomenology,[17] except that the focus of phenomenology tends to be the listener's perceptions, while the focus of my analyses will be the relationship between what the jazz musician hears and how this affects his or her improvisation—the two concerns are not perfectly concentric.

Much has been written about individual jazz musicians' improvisations; however, the musical effects of interaction between improvisers has not received much attention. Notable exceptions include the writings of Paul Rinzler, Paul Berliner, and Ingrid Monson. Each of these authors describes and analyzes musical interaction between players in jazz performance. In "Preliminary Thoughts on Analyzing Musical Interaction among Jazz Performers," Rinzler lists five types of common interactions, including: (1) "call and response," which he describes as musical dialogue between equals; (2) "fills," which he says are similar to call and response, except that in this case a musician briefly emerges from the background of the performance to respond to the foreground soloist's improvisation; (3) "accenting the end of formal units," which he describes as a coordination between the soloist and rhythm section to mark structural boundaries; (4) "common motive," which he says involves the "exact repetition of a phrase"; and (5) "responding to the 'peaks' of the soloist," which he describes as the rhythm section's support of the overall level of intensity of a soloist's improvisation.[18] Whereas this list does indeed describe some common ways that jazz musicians interact, Rinzler seems to view these interactions as isolated techniques that the musicians occasionally draw upon and incorporate into a performance. In contrast, I will be viewing interaction as something more elemental, as more of a continual musical process that is incorporated into the very fabric of the performance, and which may, at times, manifest itself in the form of "fills" or "call and response," but which may also involve much subtler kinds of interactions, involving, say, the relationship between a soloist's improvised melody and a pianist's chord voicings, or the effect of a drummer's rhythmic patterns on a soloist. In other words, by viewing a jazz performance in terms of the model of the improvisational process that I have outlined above, anything played by any member of the ensemble can potentially have an effect on any other member of the ensemble, increasing the range of possibilities for potential interactions far beyond those described in Rinzler's list.

Berliner and Monson take a more ethnomusicological approach in their works. Berliner's *Thinking in Jazz* is a comprehensive and appropriately ethnographic work, focusing on the role of the jazz community in a jazz musician's acquisition of skills as a soloist and ensemble player.[19] In *Saying Something*, Monson's goal is to show the relationships and similarities between musical interaction and cultural or social interaction.[20] She interviews musicians, analyzes the metaphors they use to describe what's happening when they perform, and maps these descriptions onto transcriptions of jazz performances. Her stated goal is to explore the concept of interaction on several levels, including: "(1) the creation of music through the improvisational interaction of sounds; (2) the interactive shaping of social networks and communities that accompany musical participation; and (3) the development of culturally variable meanings and ideologies that inform the interpretation of jazz in American society" (2). Monson begins with an examination of mediated social and cultural practices, and then looks for analogous principles in jazz performances. This book complements Monson's social and cultural emphasis by focusing on performance as an immanent experience. It will examine and explore the interactive musical processes between improvising musicians that contribute to the generation of a jazz performance.

The analysis of Cannonball Adderley's improvisation at the beginning of this chapter briefly touches upon these issues. First, the improvisation was considered in isolation and described in detail. Questions were then raised as to the reason for a drastic change in the style of the improvisation. The improvised line itself did not really supply any answers to these questions, but an examination of Wynton Kelly's simultaneous improvisation suggested a strong possibility: Adderley's change of style was in response to Kelly's fleeting reference to that style. A further example demonstrates more interaction between the players, but in the opposite direction—this time, a motive played by Adderley influences Kelly's improvised accompaniment. Thus, the analysis moved from a consideration of the *product* (the improvisation and its transcription) to a deduction of the interactive *processes* that influenced its creation.

These issues are examined in more detail over the course of this work. In the remainder of this chapter, each member of the rhythm section will be considered, as will common relationships and interactions between various combinations of rhythm section members and the soloist. We will see that, even though the interaction between musicians can have a strong influence over how each musician realizes his or her part, musicians are not *entirely* free to improvise whatever they want; rather, they each fulfill certain prescribed roles within the ensemble and for the most part improvise within the constraints of these roles. Chapter 2, "Harmony and Interaction," will explore the process of harmonic negotiation that takes place in a small-group jazz performance, examining ways that the interaction between musicians can alter or modify the realization of a tune's harmonic progression. Chapter 3, "Form and Interaction," will examine ways that musicians play within predefined phrase structures and interact to negotiate the definition of formal boundaries. Finally, Chapter 4, "Breaking Down the Boundaries: Steps toward Free Jazz," will explore performances that connect bebop and free jazz by breaking down the constraining factors of prescribed ensemble roles, predefined harmonic progressions, and predetermined formal structures that were examined in Chapters 1–3. We will see that breaking down these constraints usually requires an increase and intensification in the interaction between players in a small jazz ensemble.

Musical Roles and Behaviors

Because the main concerns of this book are the ways in which jazz musicians communicate and interact in performance as well as the ways in which these interactions affect each musician's improvisation, it's necessary to define the normative performance roles and behaviors of each musician in a small jazz group. Defining these roles will provide a basis for comparison; in order to discover and point out heightened levels of interaction, one must first understand the usual ways that standard jazz performance practice controls and allows for these interactions. It's important to note that the following descriptions of the roles and behaviors in jazz performance are not rules or laws, but are the result of an informal agreement within the jazz community. This informal agreement allows for musicians who have never played together to perform without rehearsal—each musician knows and understands his or her normative role, and knows that if each participant fulfills their role, the performance will cohere.[21]

Figure 1.19 contains a transcription of an excerpt from Charlie Parker's recording of his composition "Now's the Time."[22] This recording provides a good example of standard jazz performance practice, and the description that follows will be used to define the normative

Figure 1.19.   "Now's the Time."

roles of each musician in a small jazz ensemble. This recording features a quintet composed of Charlie Parker (alto saxophone), Miles Davis (trumpet), Dizzy Gillespie (piano),[23] Curly Russell (bass), and Max Roach (drums). To respect the copyright provisions for "Now's the Time," the composed melody is not fully notated; after the opening motive (which begins with the pick-up to m. 9), only the rhythm of the melody is notated. The remainder of the performance in this excerpt (the piano, bass, and drum parts and the improvised saxophone melody) is included.[24]

In standard jazz performance practice, a small group usually divides into two subgroups, the *front line* and the *rhythm section*. These

Figure 1.19. (continued)

two subgroups divide up the musical responsibilities: the front line is usually responsible for the melody, whereas the rhythm section provides and defines the harmony and rhythm. These divisions are, of course, not absolute; the front line's melodies often contribute to the overall harmony and rhythm of the performance, and the rhythm section's harmony and rhythm often have melodic aspects or effects. Nevertheless, the division, however crude, serves a useful purpose: it symbolizes the group aesthetic of jazz, an aesthetic that values both the division of labor and the sharing of responsibilities. In this particular performance, the front line consists of saxophone

Figure 1.19. (continued)

and trumpet, and the rhythm section is made up of piano, bass, and drums. The specific instrumentation of a small jazz ensemble may vary—the front line might consist of only a saxophone or a trumpet, it might include a trombone or additional saxophonists, the rhythm section might have a guitarist in addition to or instead of a pianist— but the group of instruments used on this recording is one of the most common in small-group jazz.

The large-scale form of this performance is determined by a standard performance practice known as the *head arrangement*. A head arrangement begins with a statement of a composed *tune* (the "head"), follows with a series of improvised solos by some or all of the members of the group, and ends with a restatement of the head.[25] In this performance,

Figure 1.19. (continued)

the head arrangement is preceded by an eight-measure introduction played by the rhythm section. After this introduction, the saxophone and trumpet enter in m. 9 with a statement of the head, in this case, Charlie Parker's twelve-bar blues composition "Now's the Time."[26] Being twelve measures long, this statement of the head extends through m. 20. The head is then followed by improvised saxophone and trumpet solos, and finally ends with a restatement of the head. The behavior of the saxophone and trumpet in this performance is standard for the front line: being primarily responsible for the melody, they play the head, improvise new melodies, and finally repeat the head to end the performance.

The primary role of the rhythm section is to accompany, support, and complement the melody of the front line by providing and defining harmony and rhythm. Reflecting the clear division of labor *between* the front line and the rhythm section, there is also a division of labor *within* the rhythm section. The three members of the rhythm section—piano, bass, and drums—cooperate and collaborate in interesting ways to define the harmony and rhythm. They do this by fulfilling three different functions: (1) the defining of the harmony, (2) the defining of regular rhythm (pulse and meter), and (3) the use of nonregular rhythmic events to support the melody or propel the music forward. No single member of the rhythm section is responsible for any one of these three functions. Instead, each player normally contributes to two of the three functions. In order to define the roles of each member of the rhythm section and the ways that they contribute to the definition of harmony and rhythm (both regular and nonregular), I'd like to examine each instrument in turn, basing my examination on the transcription in figure 1.19.

The Bassist

The role of the bass in the rhythm section is both rhythmic and harmonic. Beginning in m. 9 of figure 1.19, the bass player provides the basic quarter-note pulse of the performance by means of a *walking bass line*, which, once begun, continues through to the end of the recording. Besides defining the basic pulse, the bassist also contributes to the realization of the harmonic progression by improvising a line that emphasizes harmonically significant pitches (usually roots, 3rds, or 5ths) on beat 1 or 3 of each measure. For example, in m. 9, the bass player plays the root of F^7 (F) on beats 1 and 2 before moving to the 3rd (A) on beats 3 and 4. Whereas the rhythmic and harmonic aspects of the bass line are the most important, its melodic aspects should not be overlooked. The bass player's improvised line not only emphasizes harmonically significant pitches on strong beats, but also connects these pitches through the use of passing and neighbor notes. In m. 10, the bass line begins on the root of $B\flat^7$, then plays a B♮ passing note that connects to C (the 5th of F^7) on the downbeat of m. 11. This process—improvising a quarter-note line that melodically connects harmonically significant pitches—continues throughout. Even though this process seems somewhat restrictive, the actual choice of which notes to play is left up to the bassist, and this choice can be influenced by the other band members' improvisations. For example, the bass player's decision to play the 7th of F^7 (E♭) on the downbeat of m. 24 may have been influenced by the fact that Charlie Parker ended his phrase on an E♭ in the previous measure. It is important to note that a bassist isn't always restricted to playing a walking bass line, but this is simply its most common, normative role in small-group jazz.

The Drummer

The drummer helps the bass player define the basic, regular rhythm by playing two different repetitive patterns: the *ride pattern* and the *backbeat*. These two patterns are notated in figure 1.20a. The ride pattern is played on the suspended cymbal—which, for this reason, is often called the "ride" cymbal. Although the ride pattern is notated as a quarter note followed by two eighths, in practice the two eighth notes are not played evenly, but are "swung"; that is, they are played unevenly—the first note longer, the second note shorter. A more rhythmically precise notation of the ride pattern might be something like that contained in figure 1.20b, although the exact relationship between the long and short notes may vary depending on a variety of factors, including tempo and style.[27] Besides the ride pattern, the drummer also plays another regular rhythmic pattern called the *backbeat*. This

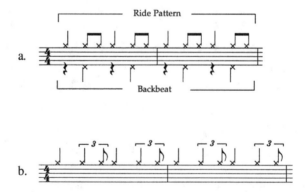

Figure 1.20. Basic drum patterns.

pattern is played on the "hi-hat," which consists of two small cymbals on a stand that are attached to a foot pedal. When the drummer presses down on the foot pedal, the two small cymbals come together, making a short, crisp, dry sound often rendered onomatopoetically by the word "chick." To play the backbeat, the drummer depresses the foot pedal on beats 2 and 4 of each measure.

In playing these two patterns, the drummer contributes to the definition of the regular rhythm of the performance: the ride pattern defines the quarter-note pulse; the backbeat helps to define the meter.[28] Although both of these patterns are played on cymbals, they sound very different; because the drummer typically allows the ride cymbal to ring, only the attack of the ride pattern is heard, and the ringing of the cymbal provides a sustained sonic backdrop for the performance. This contrasts with the short, percussive sound of the hi-hat backbeat that overlays the ride pattern. The result is that the ride pattern creates a sense of continuity, flow, and forward motion, whereas the backbeat segments that flow into metrically emphasized units and acts as an undertow, generating tension within the forward flow. Returning to figure 1.19, the drummer establishes both the backbeat and ride pattern immediately in the introduction, and continues them throughout the entire performance.

Besides contributing to the regular rhythmic pulse and meter, the drummer also supports the melody and improvisations of the front line by playing nonregular rhythms on the snare drum, tom-toms, bass drum, or crash cymbal. Typically, the drummer does this in one of three ways: (1) by *reacting* to the front line, (2) by *coordinating* or *locking up* with the front line, or (3) by *anticipating* or *setting up* the front line's melody or improvisation. Figure 1.21 contains the drum part and the front line melody of mm. 9–20. In this figure, the drummer provides all three types of rhythmic support. In mm. 9, 10, and 12, the drummer *reacts* to the front line by hitting the snare drum immediately after the melody reaches each quarter-note resting point. These accented, syncopated rhythms provide a rhythmic vitality that propels the music forward. In the first two measures of the second four-bar phrase (mm. 13 and 14), the drummer plays the same rhythm as the previous phrase, but this time, because the melody is one note longer, the

Figure 1.21. "Now's the Time," front line and drums, mm. 9–20.

drummer and the front line *lock up*. Even though the overall musical effect is similar to the first phrase—that is, the music is propelled forward—the relationship between the front line and the drummer is one of coordination and cooperation, rather than reaction. In mm. 16 and 18, the drummer *sets up* the syncopated entrance of the melody by hitting the snare drum squarely on the beat. In these measures, it's the front line's syncopated entrance that provides the rhythmic vitality, but the drummer contributes to this vitality by providing a frame of reference (the squarely on-the-beat quarter-note snare-drum hit) that sets off and defines the syncopated entrance of the front line.

The Pianist

The role of the pianist in the rhythm section, like that of the bassist, is both rhythmic and harmonic. The pianist contributes to the definition of harmony and rhythm by comping[29]—that is, by playing chord voicings that define the harmonic progression of the tune in a rhythmic, often syncopated manner. After the eight-measure introduction, the pianist comps throughout, for instance, as in figure 1.19. The rhythmic placement of the pianist's chords is nonregular, and these chords interact with the front line in ways analogous to that of the drummer's snare drum. In other words, the pianist reacts to, locks up with, or sets up the melodies of the front line.

Musical Relationships within the Rhythm Section

As discussed earlier, the three members of the rhythm section support the front line by defining the harmony, the regular rhythm, and nonregular rhythmic events. The preceding descriptions of the normative role of each member of the rhythm section do not give the complete picture, however. To gain a more complete understanding of how a rhythm section works, it's necessary to explore the network of relationships between the players. Figure 1.22 presents a schematic of these relationships. The lines connecting each pair of instruments show that each pair works together to define one of the three parameters. I'd like to briefly consider each pair of instruments and examine how they collaborate.

Bass and Piano

Figure 1.23 contains the bass and piano parts from mm. 9–12 of "Now's the Time." As diagrammed in figure 1.22, these two instruments work

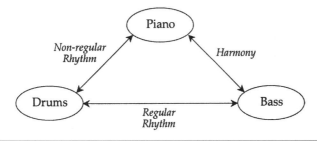

Figure 1.22. Schematic of relationships within rhythm section.

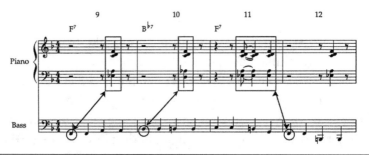

Figure 1.23. "Now's the Time," piano and bass, mm. 9–12.

together to define the harmony of the tune. In m. 9, the bassist plays the root and 3rd of the chord F^7, and the pianist plays a voicing that contains the root, 3rd, 5th, 7th, and 13th. In m. 10, the pianist's voicing of Bb^7 contains the 3rd, 5th, 7th, and 9th, but does not contain the root. The bassist, however, does provide it, so that between the pianist and bassist the complete Bb^7 is spelled out. Because there is a certain amount of flexibility in the realization of the harmonic progression, the bassist and pianist must always listen to each other in order to effectively and musically define the harmony. Chapter 2 explores the ways that interaction between the piano, bass, and front line affects the realization of the harmonic progression.

Bass and Drums

Figure 1.24 contains the bass and drum parts from mm. 9–12 of "Now's the Time." As seen in the diagram of figure 1.22, these two instruments work together to define the regular rhythm (i.e., the pulse and meter) of the performance. The walking bass line and the ride pattern both provide the basic quarter-note pulse, and the hi-hat's backbeat helps to define the meter. In order for the performance to

Figure 1.24. "Now's the Time," bass and drums, mm. 9–12.

"swing," the drummer and bassist must listen intently to each other and coordinate their rhythmic patterns.

In the abstract, these rhythmic patterns played by the bassist and drummer are very simple, but when one considers the *way* that the musicians play these rhythms and how this contributes to the feeling of swing, things get more complex. Returning to "Motion and Feeling through Music," Charles Keil examines this issue in some depth, exploring the subsyntactical aspects of the relationship between bassists and drummers (341–344). He argues that the swing, or "vital drive"[30] of a jazz performance is created when the bassist and drummer pull against an underlying pulse, playing their rhythms either slightly ahead of or slightly behind the beat. Keil creates a taxonomy of both bassists and drummers, based on their relationship to the underlying pulse. He describes drummers as falling into two distinct groups: those who play "on top" of the beat, and those who "lay back" behind it (341). He makes a similar distinction between two basic styles of bass playing, defining one as "chunky"—that is, heavy, percussive, drumlike, on or ahead of the beat—and the other as "stringy," which he describes as light, sustained, slightly behind the beat (343).

Keil considers a number of different combinations of bassists and drummers from various jazz ensembles. He describes Thelonious Monk's 1958 rhythm section as consisting of a "chunky" bassist (Ahmed Abdul Malik) and an "on-top" drummer (Roy Haynes); he likewise describes Miles Davis's 1956 and 1965 rhythm sections (bassists Paul Chambers and Ron Carter, drummers Philly Joe Jones and Tony Williams, respectively) as combinations of a "stringy" bassist and a "lay-back" drummer. Although this examination of the extremely subtle aspects of how the rhythm section musicians play their parts is interesting, insightful, and supports Keil's argument that jazz is more about process than syntax, I feel that it yields mixed results. While Keil criticizes scholars such as Meyer who ignore the subtle, subsyntactical rhythmic aspects of music, he himself overgeneralizes and simplifies the subject by categorizing individual players into one of two groups, ignoring the fact that, in performance, bassists and drummers can change the way they play, modifying the placement of their rhythms in relationship to the beat in response to the musical circumstances. For example, drummer Tony Williams, whom Keil describes as a "lay-back" drummer, actually has an extremely flexible and dynamic approach to rhythm, with the ability to place his rhythmic patterns ahead of, behind, or squarely on the beat.[31] Likewise, bassist Paul Chambers, whom Keil describes as a "stringy" bassist, also can change the relationship of his bass line to an underlying pulse. In the Miles Davis Quintet's performance of "Blues by Five,"[32] for example, Chambers begins Davis's solo in a relaxed manner, playing "in the pocket"—that is, just slightly behind the beat. As the performance progresses, John Coltrane begins to improvise, and as he builds the level of intensity throughout his solo, Chambers responds by closing the gap between his bass line and the underlying beat, moving more toward playing in the "chunky" style. In doing so, Chambers contributes to the increase in energy and intensity that Coltrane creates in his improvised solo.

Piano and Drums

Figure 1.25 returns to the performance of "Now's the Time," showing the piano and drum parts for mm. 9–12. In mm. 9, 10, and 12, the pianist and drummer lock up—that is, they both respond the same way to the front line melody. While the pianist and drummer play exactly the same rhythm in this example, this will not always be the case. Rather, the pianist and drummer share a musical function: to provide nonregular rhythmic events in response to, or in support of, the front line. Throughout the remainder of the example in figure 1.19, the pianist and drummer sometimes play the same rhythms, and sometimes do not. On the occasions that the pianist and drummer do lock up their rhythms, the effect is one of increased rhythmic vitality and drive.

Figure 1.25 "Now's the Time," piano and drums, mm. 9–12.

In "Now's the Time," the pianist and drummer lock up their rhythms in response to the melody; but it is also possible for this kind of interaction to go the other way, that is, the pianist and drummer might create an increase in musical intensity by coordinating their rhythms, which in turn may affect the way that a soloist improvises over their accompaniment. Just such an interaction takes place during trumpeter Nat Adderley's solo on the Cannonball Adderley Quintet's performance of "Spontaneous Combustion."[33] Throughout the first part of his solo, Nat Adderley usually improvises simple, "bluesy" melodies composed of short, repetitive, rifflike figures. The musical effect created by this style of improvisation is one of relative stasis; the short, repetitive figures do not create a strong feeling of forward motion toward a musical goal. Approximately halfway through Nat Adderley's solo, pianist Bobby Timmons sets up a new chorus by playing the strong rhythmic pattern transcribed in figure 1.26a. Timmons uses this pattern to signal a syncopated rhythmic pattern with which he continues his accompaniment at the beginning of the next chorus. With this syncopated pattern, which is transcribed in figure 1.26b, Timmons creates a tremendous feeling of forward motion by continually anticipating the strong beats (beats 1 and 3) by one half of a beat, placing his accented voicings on the second half of beats 2 and 4. As shown in figure 1.26c, drummer Louis Hayes, having heard Timmons's signal in the previous two measures, responds immediately, locking up with Timmons's rhythms.[34]

This coordination between Timmons and Hayes further heightens the rhythmic intensity and strong sense of forward motion, and soloist Nat Adderley responds by changing the way he improvises. Figure 1.27 combines the transcription of Timmons's and Hayes's rhythmic patterns with Adderley's improvised response. In contrast to the short, repetitive, non-goal-oriented melodies he improvised earlier in the solo, Adderley responds to the rhythm section's strong feeling of forward motion by improvising a melody that itself flows strongly forward. His fast, ascending sixteenth-note scale rushes to its peak, and Adderley follows this opening gesture with a long descending line that flows all the way to the downbeat of m. 5. At this point, the tension and energy created by the rhythm section are resolved, and everything returns to normal: pianist Timmons returns to playing

Piano

Figure 1.26a.   "Spontaneous Combustion," piano comping pattern.

Piano

Figure 1.26b.   "Spontaneous Combustion," piano comping continued into new chorus.

Piano

Drums

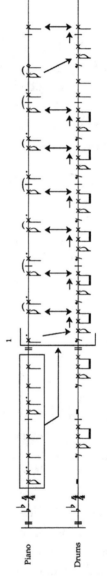

Figure 1.26c.   "Spontaneous Combustion," lock-up between piano and drums.

Figure 1.27. "Spontaneous Combustion," trumpet solo with piano and drum rhythms.

sparse, syncopated voicings, drummer Hayes reverts to occasional rhythmic interjections, and Adderley returns to improvising simpler, less goal-oriented melodies.

Summary

This chapter describes small-group jazz performance as a complex interactive process. The basic, normative roles of each member of the ensemble are defined, as are common interactions between players. A general model of jazz improvisation, based on ideas of Jean-Jacques Nattiez, is proposed; this model defines the jazz musician as being simultaneously a listener, composer, and performer. That is, each musician improvises (improvisation being a combination of composition and performance), hears the other musicians' simultaneous improvisations, and adapts or modifies his or her improvisations based on what he or she hears. A more specific example of this model may help to clarify this process. In the case of the pianist, his or her basic role in small-group jazz is to comp—that is, to accompany the front line by playing the harmony of the tune in a rhythmic manner. There are a number of factors that influence the way that the pianist chooses to fulfill this role. The pianist must listen to the bassist and the drummer to hear the basic pulse and meter, must listen to the front line and the drummer to decide when to play the chords, and must listen to the bassist and the front line to decide how to voice the chords. In other words, what the pianist hears from the other musicians can (and should) have a very strong effect on what he or she plays. The opposite is also true, namely, what the pianist plays can have a very strong effect on how each of the other musicians fulfill their roles. The analysis of Cannonball Adderley's performance of "Groovin' High" demonstrated both of these possibilities: first, Wynton Kelly's comping affected Adderley's improvisation, then Adderley's improvisation affected Kelly's comping. This work will continue to explore the interactions between the players in small-group jazz by examining several transcribed jazz performances and will examine the ways that these interactions between players can affect each individual musician's improvisation.

2

HARMONY AND INTERACTION

Figure 2.1 is a lead sheet for the composition "Knows the Thyme," which is similar in many ways to Charlie Parker's composition "Now's the Time." Consisting of only a melody and chord symbols, it is a typical example of a lead sheet; it provides a melodic/harmonic framework for the musicians to work within in performance. In its simplest form, a performance of "Knows the Thyme" would involve interactions like those we encountered in the analysis of the Charlie Parker Quintet's performance of "Now's the Time" in chapter 1: the bassist would define and connect the roots of chords, the pianist would fill out harmonies in a rhythmic manner, and the front line would either play the composed melody or improvise new ones. While this description of the performance process is an oversimplification—we will see later in the chapter that the lead sheet itself cannot be taken as a fixed entity—it will give us a place to start our examination of the processes that musicians use to create a performance.

When performing a jazz composition such as "Knows the Thyme" (or "Now's the Time"), each musician has a great deal of leeway in how they interpret the chord symbols on the lead sheet. For example, the first chord symbol in figure 2.1 is F^7. While the symbol "F^7" denotes a very specific harmony—one made up of the pitches F, A, C, and E♭—this harmony may be realized in any number of ways. The soloist may improvise a line based on: (1) the pitches of the chord designated by the symbol (in this case F–A–C–E♭); (2) major/perfect "upper extensions," including the major 9th G, perfect 11th B♭, or major 13th D; (3) chromatically altered upper extensions, including the flatted-9th G♭, sharped-9th G♯, sharped-11th B♮, or flatted-13th D♭; or (4) conjunct passing and neighbor motions connecting or embellishing each of these pitches. Figure 2.2 collates all of these possibilities into a near-complete chromatic scale above the F^7 harmony.

Figure 2.1. Lead sheet for "Knows the Thyme."

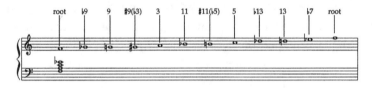

Figure 2.2. F^7 harmony with chord tones and extensions.

In practice, improvisers will rarely use all of these pitches within a single solo, but will pick and choose from among them to construct their lines. In fact, individual musicians tend to make fairly consistent choices with regard to which pitches they choose and how they choose to connect them; it is this consistency that, in part, gives a particular musician an identifiable sound, a scalar thumbprint.

As an example of the ways that musicians create an identifiable melodic profile by realizing harmonic progressions in a consistent way, I would like to compare the first choruses of both Charlie Parker's and Miles Davis's improvised solos from the recording of "Now's the Time" discussed in the previous chapter.[1] From these choruses, transcribed in figure 2.3, we can see and hear that these two musicians realize these harmonies very differently. Figure 2.3 aligns their two solos and places the chord symbols in between; the arabic numerals below each part identify upper extensions and other prominent, harmony-defining pitches. Not all of the pitches have numbers beneath them; I have chosen to designate those pitches that are emphasized in some way, possibly because they begin or end a gesture, because they receive an agogic or metric accent, or because they are highlighted by the contour of the improvised line.

Figure 2.3.   Parker's and Davis's improvisations on "Now's the Time."

Parker (upper staff) tends to improvise florid lines emphasizing roots, 3rds, 5ths, and 7ths, while using other diatonic and chromatic notes to embellish and connect these pitches. In his first phrase, mm. 1–4, he strongly emphasizes F, A, and C—the root, 3rd, and 5th of the tonic F⁷—ignoring the alteration of A♮ to A♭ that would be needed to fully define B♭⁷ in m. 2. In m. 3, he ends his phrase by leaping an augmented 4th from A to E♭, completing the F⁷ harmony and bringing to the foreground the tension that this dissonant interval lends to the underlying harmony. In ending his phrase this way, Parker leaves us hanging, awaiting the resolution of the tension caused by this dissonant interval. As a result, the music feels propelled forward into the next phrase, where the pianist and bassist resolve this tension by playing B♭⁷ in m. 5. In his second phrase, mm. 5–8, Parker *does* make the change from A♮ to A♭, which serves as both a 7th of B♭⁷ in mm. 5–6 as well as a flatted "blue" 3rd over the F⁷ in m. 7. Parker completes this phrase with a fast flourish that leads to the root of D^7 in m. 8. In his third phrase, mm. 9–12, Parker briefly increases the level of harmonic tension by using more "colorful" pitches that clash with the basic notes of the underlying harmony: on the first beat of the C^7 harmony, he plays D♭, or the flatted-9th, which clashes with the root C; through beats 3 and 4, he sustains an A, the 13th, which clashes with both the 5th G and the 7th B♭. He begins m. 11 by playing G, the 9th, which clashes with the root F and the 3rd A of F^7, and finally resolves this tension on beat 2 by ending on the root F.

In contrast to Parker's emphasis on basic chord tones, Davis (lower staff in figure 2.3) chooses to emphasize more "colorful" pitches. In fact, by continually emphasizing upper extensions such as 9ths, sharped-11ths, and 13ths, Davis seems to invert the usual relationship between consonance and dissonance. Generally we think of dissonant pitches as playing a subsidiary role, serving to embellish and connect consonant ones; in this improvisation, however, Davis tends to use consonant pitches to embellish and connect more dissonant, "colorful" pitches; I have designated these consonant embellishing pitches in the figure by placing parentheses around their arabic numerals. In m. 2, Davis embellishes a sustained G, the 13th of B♭^{7}, with the lower neighbor F, the 5th. Moving into m. 3, he again embellishes G—heard here as the 9th above F^7—with an upper neighbor A, the 3rd. After leaping up to the 13th D on the second half of beat 2, Davis leaps down to the sharped-11th B and then proceeds to fill the gap between them with the passing note C, a consonant 5th, which leads back up to D, the 13th, on which he ends the phrase. In his second phrase, he continues to give priority to upper extensions: he begins by emphasizing E, the sharped-11th over B♭^{7}, in m. 5 before again ascending through a consonant passing note—the 5th F—to the dissonant 13th G in m. 6. His emphasis on G continues through m. 7, where it again is heard as a 9th above F^7. In mm. 8–9, the tension briefly subsides when Davis emphasizes the more consonant pitches A (the 5th of D^7), and G (the root of G^{-7}). But this respite is only temporary: he ends his chorus in m. 11 by emphasizing the dissonant pitches E and G, the natural-7th and 9th above F^7, and, once again, he fills in the gap between these pitches with a more consonant passing F, the root.

The musical effect of the two different improvisations demonstrated in this figure is interesting; Parker's constant emphasis on roots, 3rds, and 7ths makes his line sound very rooted in, and generated from, the underlying harmonic progression, while Davis's emphasis on upper extensions "separates" his improvisation from the harmony provided by the rhythm section, creating a feeling of musical stratification. In fact, if Davis's first phrase was heard in isolation—that is, without the accompaniment provided by the rhythm section—it would be very difficult to argue that his melody conveys the harmonic progression of the first phrase of an F blues; indeed, with its strong emphasis on G, B♮, and D, it seems to more strongly convey the key of G rather than F. Furthermore, the way these musicians balance their choice of harmonic pitches with the quality of their improvised musical gestures is also interesting: Parker tends to emphasize simpler harmonic resources (roots, 3rds, 5ths, and 7ths), while improvising more complex, florid melodic gestures; Davis, on the other hand, improvises much simpler melodic shapes, but chooses more colorful, tension-filled pitches to create these shapes. For example, in the first three measures of his second phrase (mm. 5–7), Parker focuses on the pitches F and A♭—which serve both as the 5th and 7th of B♭^{7} and the root and flatted-3rd of F^7—but emphasizes these limited, basic pitch resources with energetic, forward-moving gestures that almost create a feeling analogous to musical "whiplash": after leaping up an octave from the initial F in m. 5, he immediately cascades down through the quick, "smeared" grace notes to A♭, before returning to F on the second half of beat 4. After sustaining the F into m. 6, he continues his line by leaping down to D before zigzagging and rushing up to A♭. In the next measure, he repeats the first part of this gesture, but after sustaining the F into m. 8, he plays a fast flourish that ultimately shoots up an octave before coming to close on the root of D^7. In these same measures, Davis emphasizes more colorful pitches—the sharped-11th in m. 5, the 13th in m. 6, and the 9th in m. 7—and uses these pitches in gestures that are much simpler than Parker's: his melody is constrained to a relatively narrow range, moves primarily by step, and, in contrast to the way Parker's melody rapidly and repeatedly traverses the distance between its upper and lower boundaries,

Figure 2.4. Gillespie's piano comping for "Now's the Time," mm. 9–20.

Davis's melody slowly and gradually works its way up from its low point, E, in m. 5 to its high point, C, in m. 7.

The pianist in a small jazz ensemble also has a great deal of freedom in choosing how to voice specific harmonies. In figure 2.4, which shows the piano comping for the first statement of the head in this performance, Dizzy Gillespie primarily voices the harmonies with basic chord tones (root, 3rd, 5th, and 7th) plus one or more additional upper extensions. For example, he voices F[7] in m. 9 with the root, 3rd, 5th, 7th, and 13th, and the Bb[7] in m. 10 with the 3rd, 5th, 7th, and 9th. In m. 20, he colorfully voices the final C[7] with the 3rd, 7th, flatted-9th, sharped-11th, and 13th. The altered upper extensions add an additional level of tension and complexity to this voicing; both the flatted-9th and the sharped-11th create dissonant intervals with the root C (not notated in the transcription but played by the bass). This tension-laden voicing of C[7] serves a structural musical function: the added dissonance (and implied need for resolution) created by the altered upper extensions helps to propel the music forward into the next chorus, where these tensions are resolved when the musicians return to F[7].[2]

Perhaps the first author to deal extensively with this subject—that is, the practice and resulting musical effect of playing different pitches

1. D♭ lydian

2. D♭ lydian augmented

3. D♭ lydian diminished

4. D♭ auxiliary diminished

5. D♭ auxiliary augmented

6. D♭ auxiliary diminished blues

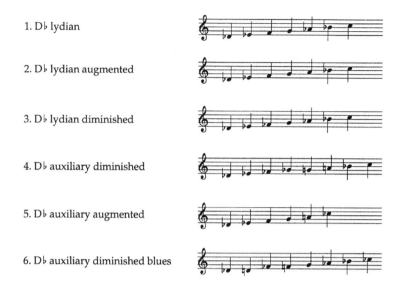

Figure 2.5.   Russell's parent D♭ lydian and related scales.

above a given harmony—is George Russell, who did so in his influential work *The Lydian Chromatic Concept of Tonal Organization*.[3] In the introduction to this work, Russell says his goal is to develop an "organization of tonal resources from which the jazz musician may draw to create his improvised lines." He compares jazz improvisation to the work of a visual artist, saying that tonal resources are "like an artist's palette: the paints and colors, in the form of scales ... [are] waiting to be blended by the improviser." More specifically, his theory operates as "a chromatic concept providing a musician with an awareness of the full spectrum of tonal colors available" (1).

Russell theorizes a relationship between chords and scales, postulating that every chord comes from a "parent" scale, which is the scale that "best conveys the quality of that chord." The example he begins with is the chord E♭7, which he says has a parent scale of D♭ lydian: this scale contains the chord tones E♭, G, B♭, and D♭, as well as the additional pitches F, A♭, and C, which serve to connect them. He then goes on to describe scales in addition to the parent scale that he says may be used "to add color to the parent scale at the discretion of the improviser" (4). Returning to his example of an E♭7 harmony, Russell says that besides the parent scale of D♭ lydian, the improviser may use the additional scales notated in figure 2.5.

Russell calls scale 2 the "lydian augmented" because it is identical to the lydian scale except for its fifth note, which is raised by a half step; therefore, the 1st, 3rd, and 5th pitches of the scale (D♭–F–A) form an augmented triad. Likewise, scale 3 is called the "lydian diminished" because it too is identical to the parent lydian scale with the exception of a minor 3rd, and because a diminished triad can be formed by combining the first, third, and (enharmonically respelled) fourth pitches (D♭–F♭–G♯/A♭♭). He calls scales 4, 5, and 6 "auxiliary," because they are not derived by altering the parent lydian scale, but rather by stringing together symmetrical patterns of intervals. Scales 4 (auxiliary diminished) and 6 (auxiliary diminished blues) are the two different possible versions of an octatonic scale—both alternate whole steps and half steps, with 4 beginning with a whole step and 6 beginning with a half step—and, in both scales, the root, 3rd, 5th, and 7th form the diminished seventh chord D♭–F♭–G–B♭. Scale 5 (auxiliary augmented) is a whole-tone scale, and its root, 3rd, and 5th form the augmented triad D♭–F–A. Russell writes that these six scales "represent the primary colors of music," and that "each scale contributes its own melodic color to the sound of the chord." Furthermore, he points out that combining these six scales results in a complete chromatic collection, which he dubs the "lydian chromatic scale," and that these scales create different paths that improvisers can take through this chromatic scale (9).

With these scales, Russell attempts to explain the way jazz musicians can control their use of the pitches of the chromatic scale in their improvisation over a given harmony. By creating a hierarchy of scales all generated from a parent scale, he defines some pitches as more "essential" (those contained in the parent scale) and others as more "colorful" (those from the other scales). Listening to Charlie Parker's and Miles Davis's improvised solos on "Now's the Time" in terms of Russell's theory, one can say that Parker tends to use the more "essential" pitches of the parent scales, while Davis tends to emphasize the more "colorful" pitches of the scales generated *from* the parent scales. Figure 2.6 compares the first four measures of Charlie Parker's (line *a*) and Miles Davis's (line *c*) improvised solos on "Now's the Time" in relation to scales generated from Russell's theory. According to Russell, the parent scale of F⁷ is E♭ lydian, which is notated under

Figure 2.6. Parker's and Davis's first improvised phrases with scales (after Russell).

Parker's solo on line *b*. Other than the occasional grace note, Parker uses the notes of this scale exclusively throughout his first phrase. Davis, on the other hand, makes use of one of the scales generated from the parent scale, specifically the scale Russell calls the lydian augmented; the E♭ lydian augmented scale is notated on line *d*, under Davis's solo. This scale contains the "colorful" pitch B♮, which Davis strongly emphasizes in m. 3.

While Russell's theory was very influential—musicians such as Miles Davis and Bill Evans publicly acknowledged its influence on their composing and improvising—in practice, the specifics of his theory end up being less important than some of the general concepts it advances. That is, his arcane, nonstandard terminology (e.g., "lydian augmented," "lydian diminished," and "auxiliary augmented" scales) and lydian-based approach were never widely adopted, but the more general concept of chord/scale relationships contributed to the historical development of modal jazz and dominates jazz pedagogy to this day.[4] As we saw in the analysis of "So What" in chapter 1, modal jazz features long stretches of music based on a single scale or mode; in the case of "So What," the performance was based on sixteen measures of D dorian, eight measures of E♭ dorian, and eight more measures of D dorian. Russell's chord/scale relationships, however, allowed musicians to conceptualize, and thus to disseminate, modal jazz and, in the process, to reconcile chord-based and scale-based approaches to jazz improvisation.

Modal jazz will be discussed further in chapter 4. For now, I would like to return to jazz performances based on chord progressions, moving beyond a consideration of the way that individual musicians realize a harmonic progression to an examination of how player interaction can affect this process.

Basic Harmonic Interaction

It is in the realization of the individual chord symbols that the most basic forms of harmonic interaction can take place. In a good jazz performance, all of the musicians will listen to each other and create their individual parts based not only on a "preset" harmonic progression, but also on how the other musicians are choosing to realize their parts. The pianist's choice of chord voicing, for instance, may influence both the soloist's and the bassist's lines, and vice versa. In figure 2.7, Dizzy Gillespie anticipates the C^7 harmony of m. 30, playing it on the "and" of the fourth beat of the previous measure.

Gillespie's voicing of C^7 recalls the voicing examined earlier in figure 2.4. He again uses the altered notes flatted-9th (D♭) and flatted-5th (G♭), this time to connect with the following chord F^7. That is, the voice-leading proceeds in two streams, traced with arrows in the example: G (root of G^{-7}) moves to G♭ (flatted-5th of C^7), which continues descending chromatically to F (root of F^7). Likewise, D (5th of G^{-7}) descends through the D♭ (flatted-9th of C^7) to C (5th of F^7). Introducing these chromatic passing notes not only smooths out the voice-leading, but, like the earlier example, the resulting dissonance also creates a sense of forward motion; the "colorful," dissonant voicing propels the music forward into the

Figure 2.7. Gillespie's piano comping, "Now's the Time," mm. 29–31.

Figure 2.8.   "Now's the Time," mm. 29–32.

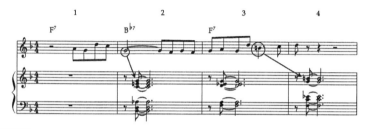

Figure 2.9.   "Now's the Time," trumpet solo mm. 1–4, with piano comping.

following measure, where the dissonance is then resolved. As shown in figure 2.8, Charlie Parker may have been influenced both by Dizzy's voicing of C7 with a flatted-9th and by the resulting chromatic voice-leading: Parker emphasizes the flatted-9th (D♭) on the downbeat of m. 30, and the primary motion of his line through the rest of the measure is motivically based on a descending half-step figure.

This example demonstrates how the pianist's choice of chord voicing can affect how the soloist chooses to improvise over that chord. In figure 2.9, the opposite occurs, namely, the soloist's impro-vised melody influences the pianist's voicing. This example is taken from Miles Davis's first improvised chorus on this same recording. In m. 2, Davis emphasizes G, the 13th of the B♭7 harmony, and Dizzy immediately responds, arranging his voicing so that G is the highest sounding pitch. Also, in m. 3, Miles plays a very "colorful" note—the sharped-11th B♮—over the F7 harmony. Dizzy hears this and again alters his voicing in m. 4 to include this colorful pitch.

"Making the Changes"

Jazz musicians use the phrase "chord changes" or the word "changes" to refer to the harmonic progression of a composition.[5] The phrase "making the changes" is used to describe a musician whose improvisation successfully negotiates the chord progression—"changes"—of a particular composition. As we have seen above, jazz musicians have a great deal of freedom in how they choose to make the changes, and each musician's choices can affect those of the other members of the group. In addition to the basic harmonic interactions described above, more complex interactions can also take place in which the musicians *alter* or *redefine* the harmonic progression over the course of the performance. In fact, more often than not, a small jazz group's performance of a composition will involve a somewhat flexible approach to the underlying changes; one of the musicians might suggest (through his or her improvisation) a substitution for a single chord or for a series of chords, and this suggestion will often be taken up by the other musicians and incorporated into the performance. The result is that the harmonic progression from a lead sheet is not necessarily a given, but rather may only be a point of departure or reference, a place in which to begin.[6]

This raises a serious question for jazz theory: What exactly are you analyzing when you analyze jazz harmony? Are you analyzing the chord progression from a lead sheet? Many sources of lead sheets—especially a very common source, *The Real Book*—are notoriously inaccurate.[7] If you do decide to analyze a harmonic progression from a lead sheet, how do you explain the differences between lead sheets for the same tune from different sources? If, on the other hand, you decide that you are going to analyze the harmony as it is played by a group of jazz musicians on a recording, another set of problems arises. Recordings of the same tune by different groups of musicians will often have similar, but not quite the same, harmonic progressions. And, even if you decide that you are going to focus your attention on only one recorded performance, the harmonic progression of that performance may still be difficult to pin down—it may change over the course of the performance, or each musician may interpret and present the harmony in a slightly different way. In other words, the difficulty (and the complexity) lies in the fact that jazz harmony is not rigid, but fluid; a given progression may change between performances or even within a single performance.[8]

How can one reconcile the disparity between different versions, both written down and performed, of the "same" harmonic progression? Does it even need to be reconciled? Some scholars criticize the effort to reconcile these variants as an attempt to force a Western ideology of coherence—and a modernist ontology of the piece—onto a music to which it doesn't really apply. But, if this kind of coherence is not a part of jazz, then why do jazz musicians talk about a soloist "making the changes," or an improvised line as either "making sense" or not? There must be *some* criteria for musical coherence.

Figuring the Blues

All of the issues mentioned above come into play when regarding the most common harmonic progression in jazz: the twelve-bar blues. The blues form is extremely malleable, existing in countless variations, yet each of these variations is identifiably "the blues." The paradox of the blues is that even though the many variations seem very different, they are somehow the same. In the effort to unravel the complexity of jazz harmony and to find its underlying coherence, I would like to begin by examining three common variants of the twelve-bar blues progression to see just *how* they are alike, yet also different. These three progressions are notated in figure 2.10.

Figure 2.10a contains what I'm calling a "basic" blues. This progression consists of only three different harmonies—F^7, Bb^7, and C^7—and has a relatively slow (and conventional) harmonic rhythm. The second variant, figure 2.10b, is slightly more complex, with an increase in the number of harmonies used as well as in the rate of harmonic change. This progression, besides being very similar to that of "Now's the Time," is the most common one used by jazz musicians, hence I am calling this the "jazz" blues progression. The third example, notated in figure 2.10c, is even more complex, with its extraordinary number of different harmonies and extremely rapid harmonic rhythm. Because this progression was famously used by Charlie Parker in his composition

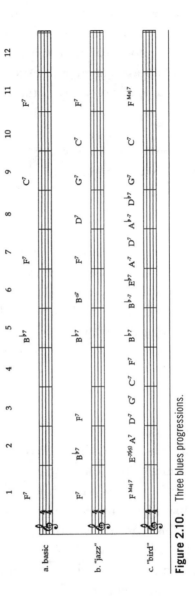

Figure 2.10. Three blues progressions.

"Blues for Alice," it is commonly known as a "bird" blues—Parker's well-known nickname was "Yardbird," or more simply, just "Bird."

Figure 2.11 maps these three variants onto one another, showing the structural similarities *between* each progression, as well as graphically representing the harmonic processes that occur *within* each progression. Significant structural harmonies have boxes around them, and the arrows, rounded-corner rectangles, and analytical beams represent dynamic relationships between harmonies, or harmonic *functions*.[9]

Line *a* contains an analysis of the "basic" blues progression. The long arcs marked *P* describe the *prolongation* of the tonic harmony F[7] over the course of the entire progression; the other two harmonies are heard in relation to this tonic. The arrow connecting B♭[7] and F[7] is marked *S*, denoting the *subdominant* function. This function describes a harmonic progression based on the root movement of an *ascending* 5th; in this case, the B♭[7] ascends a 5th to F[7]. The C[7] and F[7] harmonies of mm. 9–12 relate to one another through the *dominant function*—a harmonic progression based on the root movement of a *descending* 5th. Because this function is by far the most common progression encountered in jazz (and perhaps all tonal music), I have chosen to graphically highlight these progressions in two ways: by beaming together the roots of the harmonies on the musical staff, and by enclosing the chord symbols in long, rounded-corner rectangles.

The vertical (and angled) lines connecting the harmonies of the progressions on lines *a* and *b* bring out similarities between these two progressions. The "jazz" blues contains the same structurally significant harmonies as the basic blues; the additional chords can be seen as interpolations. The subdominant function connecting B♭[7] and F[7] in mm. 2 and 3 can be seen as an additional, smaller-scale iteration of the one connecting mm. 5 and 7. The B°[7] in m. 6 is in parentheses because it is not a "function-derived" harmony, but rather arises from voice leading—the B♮ root is a chromatic passing note connecting B♭ (the root of the B♭[7]) with C (the 5th of F[7]). Finally, the dominant progression connecting C[7] and F[7] is expanded into a continuous series of dominant progressions. This *chain* of dominant functions creates forward motion; the stream of harmonies beginning with D[7] flows strongly to the final tonic F[7].

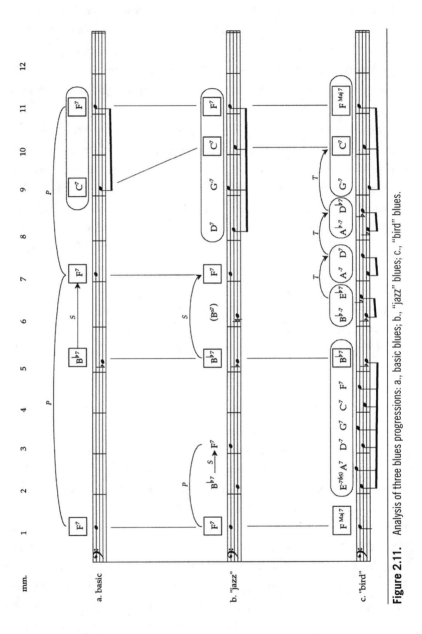

Figure 2.11. Analysis of three blues progressions: a., basic blues; b., "jazz" blues; c., "bird" blues.

The chaining together of dominant functions is used even more extensively in line *c*, the "bird" blues. The stream of harmonies beginning with $E^{-7(\flat 5)}$ in m. 2 leads very strongly to the structural $B\flat^7$ in m. 5. In the next measure, another harmonic stream begins on $B\flat^{-7}$, this time leading all the way to the final F^7. This stream is more complex than a simple chain of dominant functions, although the overall effect is still one of strong forward motion. Measures 6–8 each contain a two-chord dominant progression, as indicated by the beams and rounded-corner rectangles, but these progressions are "nested" within a larger harmonic stream, designated by the series of curved arrows, each marked with the letter T.[10] These curved arrows designate the harmonic function of the *tritone substitution*, which is similar to, and derived from, the dominant function.

Before explaining exactly how the tritone substitutions are used in this example, it may be worthwhile to explore exactly why the tritone substitution *is* similar to, and derived from, the dominant function. In jazz harmony, for the most part, three elements define a given chord: the root, 3rd, and 7th. The 5th, as we have seen in figure 2.7, may be altered or even dispensed with without changing the basic identity of the chord. In figure 2.12, these three "essential" pitches are notated for the chord symbol C^7: C is the root, E is the major 3rd, and $B\flat$ is the minor 7th. In this chord, as in all dominant-seventh chords, the interval formed between the 3rd and the 7th is a tritone.[11] This interval's dissonance makes the chord feel unstable—in need of resolution—and through this need for resolution of the instability, the chord imparts a feeling of forward motion.[12]

Besides being dissonant, the interval of a tritone is also symmetrical. Counting in semitones, it evenly divides the octave in half; the result is that its inversion is still a tritone. Figure 2.13 demonstrates this: inverting E and $B\flat$ (3rd and 7th of C^7) and respelling $B\flat$ as $A\sharp$ yields

Figure 2.12. Voicing of C^7 with root, 3rd, and 7th.

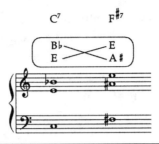

Figure 2.13.   Chords with shared pitches.

Figure 2.14.   Resolution of each chord to F⁷.

an enharmonically equivalent tritone that can serve as the major 3rd (A♯) and minor 7th (E) of F♯⁷.

It is this substitution of a dominant-seventh chord's root with the note that lies a tritone away—in this case F♯ for C—that is referred to by the term "tritone substitution." In this case—and this is a crucial point—the tritone substitute F♯⁷ does not reorient the music to a B (or B⁷) tonic, but rather maintains the same referent—F⁷—of the C⁷ dominant it replaced. Figure 2.14 shows how both of these harmonies can resolve to the F⁷ tonic, and that, furthermore, the voice-leading of the 3rds and 7ths is preserved: in both cases, E descends to E♭, B♭/A♯ descends to A♮.

This is the crucial and radical fact about the tritone substitution: not the substitution per se, which is a mere harmonic trick of the light, but its role as an enriched, intensified dominant in the original tonal context. Figure 2.15 chains all twelve dominant-seventh chords together in two different ways: in *a*, the chords progress through the dominant function, and in *b* the chords progress through the tritone substitution function. Again, although they are spelled differently, the chains of 3rds and 7ths in the upper staff of both *a* and *b* are enharmonically equivalent, and both streams of dissonant tritones propel the music forward in a similar way.[13]

a. Chain of dominant functions.

| G⁷ | C⁷ | F⁷ | B♭⁷ | E♭⁷ | A♭⁷ | D♭⁷ | F#⁷ | B⁷ | E⁷ | A⁷ | D⁷ | G⁷ |

b. Chain of tritone substitution functions.

$$G^7 \xrightarrow{T} G\flat^7 \xrightarrow{T} F^7 \xrightarrow{T} E^7 \xrightarrow{T} E\flat^7 \xrightarrow{T} D^7 \xrightarrow{T} D\flat^7 \xrightarrow{T} C^7 \xrightarrow{T} B^7 \xrightarrow{T} B\flat^7 \xrightarrow{T} A^7 \xrightarrow{T} A\flat^7 \xrightarrow{T} G^7$$

Figure 2.15. Dominant and tritone substitution functions.

Figure 2.16. Equivalence of C#⁷(♭5) and F#⁷(♭5).

It is because of this shared dissonance and resulting feeling of forward motion that a dominant-seventh chord can be used interchangeably with the one that lies a tritone away, and I am defining the *tritone substitution* function as the movement of a dominant-seventh chord downward by a half step.[14]

Additional ambiguity arises when the 5th of a dominant-seventh chord is flatted, as can be seen in figure 2.16. Here, a C⁷ is altered by lowering the 5th from G to G♭. If we respell the G♭ and B♭ as F# and A#, respectively, and then invert the chord, we end up with the same quality of chord—a dominant-seventh with a flatted-5th—transposed a tritone away. Musicians will often take advantage of this ambiguity to generate richly colorful chord voicings, or to revel in referentless ambiguity.[15] Figure 2.17 revisits Dizzy Gillespie's voicing of a C⁷ harmony that was discussed earlier. In this voicing, the upper four notes are enharmonically equivalent to an F#⁷ harmony. It is only

Figure 2.17. Alternate interpretation of $C^{7(\flat5\flat9)}$.

because of the context (both the pianist and the bass are playing C as the lowest sounding pitch) that the chord voicing is identified—somewhat baroquely—as $C^{7(\flat5\flat9)}$.

Returning to the analysis of the "Bird" blues in figure 2.11, the curved arrows in mm. 6–10 show a chain of T functions—$E\flat^7$ slides down to D^7, which slides down to $D\flat^7$, which slides down to C^7, which then moves through the dominant function to the tonic F^7. And, each of these chords in this large-scale progression is also preceded by the chord functioning as its dominant, resulting in nested harmonic progressions.

Generating Jazz Harmony

This analysis of the three blues variants serves a number of purposes. First, it points out structural similarities between the progressions—true to the whole practice of jazz improvisation, the "jazz" and "bird" blues can be seen as more elaborate versions of the "basic" blues rather than something entirely different. The analysis also defines a set of harmonic processes, or functions, that are used to explain chords interpolated between significant structural harmonies. I would like to use the insights gained from this analysis to propose a *generative* theory of jazz harmony—a theory that describes the process of generating a jazz harmonic progression. In order to develop this theory, I am going to borrow some ideas from linguistics, namely, the concepts of *deep*, *shallow*, and *surface* structures. In *Cartesian Linguistics*, Noam Chomsky writes that these concepts allow us to acknowledge that language has both an "inner and an outer aspect." He observes that "a sentence can be studied from the point of view of how it expresses a thought or from the point of view of its physical shape." In other words:

We can distinguish the 'deep structure' of a sentence from its 'surface structure.' The former is the underlying abstract structure that determines its semantic interpretation; the latter, the superficial organization of units which determines the phonetic interpretation and which relates to the physical form of the actual utterance, to its perceived or intended form.[16]

Having defined deep and surface structures, Chomsky goes on to describe the relationship between them, saying that a surface structure is generated from a deep structure through a process that can be modeled with a set of rules—a "transformational grammar"—that may vary depending on the language being spoken. Furthermore, these rules allow for a theoretically infinite number of surface structures to be generated from a single underlying deep structure, and linguists have come to describe this infinite set of possible realizations as a sentence's "shallow structure."[17]

Alan Perlman and Daniel Greenblatt draw a similar comparison between music and linguistics in their article "Miles Davis Meets Noam Chomsky: Some Observations on Jazz Improvisation and Language Structure," although their discussion focuses on the generation of improvised melodies rather than harmonic progressions.[18] Perlman and Greenblatt define the deep structure of jazz improvisation as "its underlying harmony, as expressed by the chord symbols found on all sheet music" (170). Their shallow structure is the range of possibilities that the improviser may play over the underlying deep structure. Finally, the surface structure is the actual improvised line played by the musician. Of course, defining the deep structure as the set of chord symbols found on sheet music (or a lead sheet, for that matter) raises all of the questions and problems discussed earlier, namely, *which* of the many possible sets of chord symbols should serve as the deep structure?

I would therefore like to redefine the deep structure of jazz harmony as a simplified abstraction, a mental map or network that lies *beneath* the chord changes. The shallow structure would then consist of all of the possible harmonic progressions that can be generated from that deep structure, and the surface structure would be one specific manifestation of such a harmonic progression. Viewing the blues analysis in figure 2.11 in terms of this theory, the basic blues progression can serve as the deep structure, and the "jazz" and "bird" blues can be interpreted as surface structures generated from this deep structure through the harmonic functions of subdominant, dominant, and tritone substitution. The shallow structure—not notated here—consists of all of the possible blues progressions that could be generated from this basic blues deep structure.

I would like to use this generative theory to examine another very common harmonic progression in jazz, the progression known as *rhythm changes*. The name "rhythm changes" acknowledges that this progression was initially derived from George Gershwin's song "I Got Rhythm." Like the blues, there is no single rhythm changes progression, but the term is applied to a large set of different, yet related, progressions. In order to understand the similarities between these different sets of progressions, I will begin by modeling the deep structure of rhythm changes and then will use harmonic functions to generate several common variations of the progression from this deep structure.

Figure 2.18 charts the harmonic deep structure of rhythm changes. This deep structure takes place within a thirty-two-bar song form consisting of four eight-bar phrases. This form is often described as an AABA form, the letters designating repetition and variety within the form—the first, second, and fourth phrases (the A sections) are the same, while the third phrase (the B section, or *bridge*) contrasts with these phrases. The deep structures I have derived for each section are fairly simple: the A sections prolong the tonic Bb^{Maj7} harmony; the bridge consists of strong motion toward the tonic.

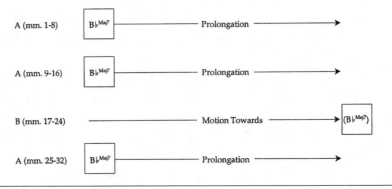

Figure 2.18.   Rhythm changes, deep structure.

Figure 2.19 shows how several common variations of the A section's harmonic progression can be generated from the deep structure. The progression in line *b* strongly prolongs the tonic by returning to it every two bars, and also each tonic is led by a stream of dominant functions: G^{-7} leads to C^{-7}, which leads to F^7, which finally returns to the tonic $B\flat^{Maj7}$. The progression in line *c* begins the same way—by returning to the tonic every two bars—but ventures a little farther afield in its second half, setting up a longer harmonic stream that, nevertheless, still leads back to the tonic. Line *d*'s progression also uses longer streams, returning to $B\flat$ every four bars, although the return to $B\flat$ in m. 5 is slightly undermined by the fact that the chord is $B\flat^7$, rather than $B\flat^{Maj7}$. This progression also introduces another harmonic function, which I am calling the *leading tone*, or *LT* function. This function, which is similar to the dominant function, provides strong forward movement by building a diminished seventh on the leading tone of a goal chord. In this progression, $B^{\circ 7}$ thus moves to C^{-7} and $C\sharp^{\circ 7}$ moves to D^{-7} through the *LT* function. The progression in line *e* is almost unrecognizable as rhythm changes, but nevertheless forms a common variant. Here, the tonic $B\flat$ only occurs once; it is set up by a long chain of dominant functions, finally arriving in m. 5. Only the relative length of the $B\flat^7$—it is a full measure long, rather than only a half measure—allows it to be identified as the most structurally significant harmony of the progression.

Figure 2.20 generates three common variants of the rhythm changes bridge, each derived from the deep structure and providing strong motion toward the tonic. The progression in line *b* is by far the most common rhythm changes bridge. It moves toward $B\flat$ by chaining together a series of dominant functions. Line *c* is similar to line *b*, but this progression strings together tritone substitutions rather than dominants. The progression in line *d* is known as the "Eternal Triangle" bridge because it was used by saxophonist Sonny Stitt in his composition of the same name. This progression is similar to the "bird" blues in its use of nested harmonic functions: the large-scale progression results from a string of tritone substitutions—E^7 leads to $E\flat^7$, which leads to D^7, and so on—and each of the chords participating in this chain is preceded by a chord derived through the dominant function.

Figure 2.19. Rhythm changes, A section, deep structure, and variants.

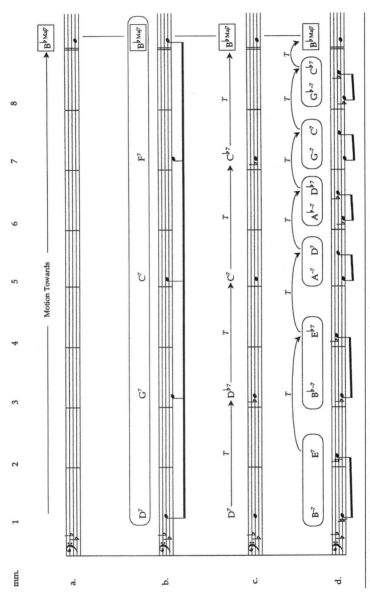

Figure 2.20. Rhythm changes, bridge, deep structure, and variants.

"Rhythm-A-Ning":
Jazz Harmony in Performance

Now that we have explored the theoretical generation of rhythm changes, I would like to examine a recorded performance of a rhythm changes composition to see just how a group of musicians work together and negotiate the precise form of this progression. The performance I am going to examine is Thelonious Monk's recording of his tune "Rhythm-A-Ning," from the album *Criss-Cross*.[19] This performance features a quartet consisting of Thelonious Monk, piano, Charlie Rouse, tenor saxophone, John Ore, bass, and Frankie Dunlop, drums. As the primary concern of my analysis is the harmonic progression, the transcriptions include the piano, saxophone, and bass parts only. Both Monk and Rouse improvise in this performance, and they both take two choruses—that is, they each improvise through two repetitions of the thirty-two-bar AABA form. I will begin by comparing several different improvised A sections, and will then turn my attention to examples of improvisations over the bridge.

Figure 2.21 contains a transcription of the first A section—that is, mm. 1–8—of Rouse's improvisation. It's difficult to determine the exact harmonic progression underlying the improvisation solely by examining the saxophone line, although, in the first four measures, Rouse strongly defines the key of B♭ major, implying the tonic as well as chords derived from the subdominant and the dominant functions, E♭⁷ and F⁷. In m. 5, he introduces an A♭, transforming the overall feel of a B♭ tonic into that of B♭⁷. Monk's skeletal piano accompaniment defines additional B♭ harmonies on the downbeat of mm. 1 and 5, but other than that does nothing to clarify the progression between these chords. The strongest definition of the harmony for this phrase lies in Ore's bass line. Listening primarily to beats 1 and 3 of each measure, a harmonic progression emerges. This progression is notated under the bass line in the example. Analyzing this progression in terms of harmonic functions shows that it has a strong similarity to the progression on line *b* in figure 2.19—the progression returns to B♭ every two measures, and each of these returns is preceded by one or more dominant functions. By returning to B♭ every two measures, this section very strongly conveys the underlying deep structure for the A section,

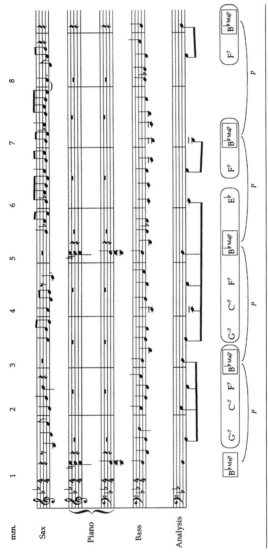

Figure 2.21. "Rhythm-A-Ning," saxophone solo, mm. 1–8.

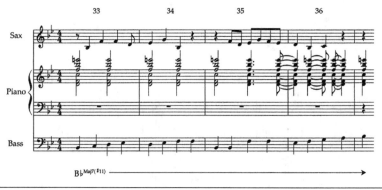

Figure 2.22. "Rhythm-A-Ning," saxophone solo, mm. 33–36.

that of prolongation of the underlying B♭ tonic harmony. This clear definition of the deep structure seems very appropriate and effective here, as this phrase begins the series of improvisations; the musicians seem to coordinate their parts to clearly present the starting point of their exploration and negotiation of the harmonic progression.

In Figure 2.22, which contains the first four measures of Rouse's second chorus (mm. 33–36 of the entire solo), Monk's piano accompaniment takes a much more active role in defining and controlling the harmonic progression. Monk plays the same chord voicing—a B♭$^{Maj9(\sharp11)}$—over and over, which has the effect of controlling and limiting the progression to that single chord. Rouse and Ore hear this and strongly emphasize this harmony in their parts. It's almost as if Monk reins in the harmony, pulling it back into the deep structure of B♭ prolongation, effectively suspending all forward motion and thus bringing the music to a standstill.

In the first four measures of the next A section (mm. 41–44, notated in figure 2.23), Monk does not play, and Rouse and Ore take advantage of this freedom by being more harmonically adventurous. Rouse begins by playing a figure that emphasizes B♭ major, and then slides up a half-step, altering the figure so that it emphasizes B major, rather than B♭. Ore is obviously listening closely, because he moves right along with Rouse, immediately shifting his bass line into the new key, before returning to B♭ in the fifth measure. The analysis underneath the example interprets this harmonic shift as a result of a tritone substitution, with the embellishing B♮ sliding down a half step, resolving to the tonic B♭.

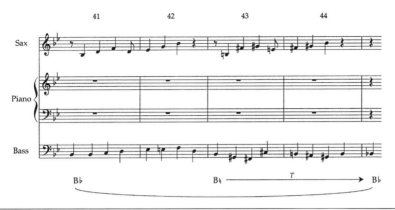

Figure 2.23. "Rhythm-A-Ning," saxophone solo, mm. 41–44.

Figures 2.24 and 2.25, which contain the first and last A sections of Monk's first improvised chorus, show two radically different realizations of the A section's deep structure. In figure 2.24, the long string of dominant functions moves through eight different dominant-seventh chords before finally arriving at the tonic B♭ in m. 5. Again, Ore goes along for the ride, immediately altering his bass line to coordinate with Monk's harmonies. This progression is similar to the one generated in line *e* of figure 2.19.

Interestingly, the musical effect of this extremely rational process of stringing together dominant functions is anything but one of rationality; on the contrary, the music feels as if it is tumbling end-over-end, spinning out of control, and rushing forward until it reaches the B♭⁷ goal, at which point everything stabilizes and returns to normal. At the return of the A section sixteen measures later (shown in figure 2.25), Monk takes a much simpler approach to the harmony. Here, the B♭ tonic returns every two measures, most often approached by a single subdominant or dominant harmony.

Figures 2.26 and 2.27 show two different realizations of the bridge's deep structure, or motion toward B♭. Figure 2.26, which is from Rouse's first chorus, moves toward the B♭ tonic by chaining dominant functions together in a manner very similar to the progression of the most common rhythm changes bridge, the one generated in line *b* of figure 2.20.

In figure 2.27, Monk, as usual, realizes this progression in a more complex way, by stringing together a combination of tritone substitutions and dominant functions.

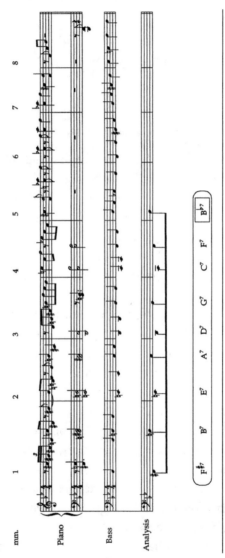

Figure 2.24. "Rhythm-A-Ning," piano solo, mm. 1–8.

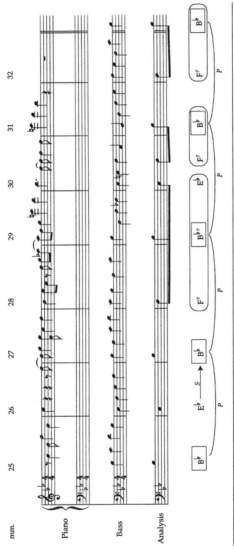

Figure 2.25. "Rhythm-A-Ning," piano solo, mm. 25–32.

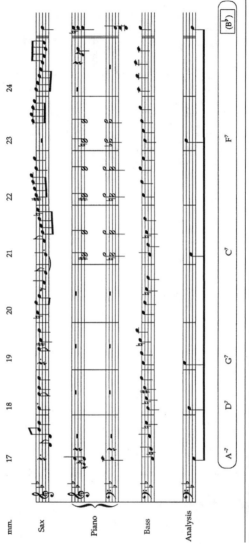

Figure 2.26. "Rhythm-A-Ning," saxophone solo, mm. 17–24.

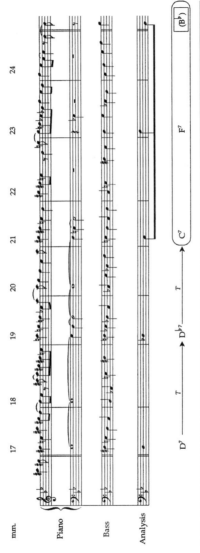

Figure 2.27. "Rhythm-A-Ning," piano solo, mm. 17–24.

Even though both of these examples are derived from the same deep structure—motion toward B♭—they feel and sound completely different. Rouse's improvisation has the feel of inevitability; his line leads us very clearly through the strongly teleological circle-of-fifths progression that results from stringing together dominant functions. In contrast, Monk's improvisation—in part, because of the sequential use of whole-tone scales—feels ambiguous and disorienting, while still creating the feeling of forward motion.

Conclusion

The analysis of "Rhythm-A-Ning" shows that, in a sense, jazz musicians literally *make* the changes in performance; that is, the specific harmonic progressions they choose to play may be flexibly realized, often changing from simple to complex within a single performance, and the precise form that these progressions take are the result of an interactive process of negotiation between the performers. Nevertheless, there is a coherence to these progressions, and this coherence comes from the fact that they are generated from a single deep structure. The generative theory I have proposed in this chapter describes ways in which jazz musicians make these changes both in composition and in performance, explaining the coherence of varied, complex harmonic progressions by showing that they can be generated from a common deep structure through the use of harmonic functions.

3

FORM AND INTERACTION

In the *New Grove Dictionary of Jazz*, Thomas Owens defines "form" as "the constructive organizing element in music, governing the presentation, development, and interrelationship of ideas."[1] Most descriptions and analyses of musical form tend to describe the large-scale organization of a piece of music—that is, the way the music is created out of smaller building blocks such as phrases or themes as well as the way these are combined into larger sections and the effect of repetition and variety both within and between these larger sections. Figure 3.1 diagrams a more or less traditional formal analysis of Charlie Parker's performance of "Now's the Time."[2] As previously discussed, this performance is a good example of a "head arrangement"; after an eight-measure introduction, a statement of the tune, or "head," is followed by a series of improvised solos, followed in turn by a final statement of the head.

Moving through this performance from beginning to end will allow us to examine and discuss the ways in which contrast and repetition contribute to its formal organization. Each section contrasts with the sections immediately before and after it: the harmonically ambiguous, unsettled feeling of the introduction (mm. 1–8) contrasts with the simple, unambiguous, riff-based melody and common harmonic progression of the head (mm. 9–20); the intricate, serpentine saxophone solo (mm. 21–56) contrasts with both the simple head that precedes it and the smooth, flowing, harmonically colorful melody of the following trumpet solo (mm. 57–80). After the trumpet solo, the rhythm section continues to play as if they were accompanying a soloist—the pianist comps, the bassist walks, and the drummer plays time—but because no one takes the lead the result is a dramatic change in texture, and thus a feeling of contrast. Immediately following this section, the horns return for a final statement of the head in mm. 93–104.

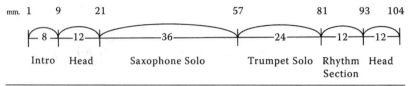

Figure 3.1.   Formal sketch, "Now's the Time."

Despite these clear contrasts, there are a number of unifying factors that tie this performance together. One of the strongest unifying forces is the relentless consistency of the rhythm section: once past the introduction, the walking bass line, piano comping, ride cymbal, and hi-hat patterns continue all the way to the end of the performance. The head arrangement itself also contributes to the coherence of the performance in a couple of ways. First, the initial head sets up the harmonic progression that will then be repeated over and over throughout the rest of the piece. Each of the following sections consists of one or more repetitions of this progression: the thirty-six-measure saxophone solo consists of three choruses, or repetitions; the twenty-four-measure trumpet solo consists of two choruses, and the section following the trumpet solo and the final head each consist of one chorus. Finally, after the intervening solo sections, the performance ends with a final statement of the head beginning in m. 93.

This return of the opening material brings the performance full circle; it's as if the head serves as a "frame" for the performance. Yet while the musicians typically play the head similarly at both the beginning and the end of the performance, the listener hears it differently each time. At the beginning of the performance, the head is new to the listener, and its purpose is to introduce the raw material (the melody, harmonic progression, and phrase structure) that will serve as the basis for the improvisations to follow. When the head returns at the end, it is no longer new to the listener; after hearing the musicians' extended exploration of its musical content, it can be heard (and understood) in a new light. By returning to the opening material and creating a frame for the performance, this final repetition of the head brings about a sense of finality and closure.

Owens's use of the word "form" to describe the organization of a jazz performance as a whole is inconsistent with jazz musicians' use of the word. Especially in small-group jazz, the long-range performance plan might be described by the musicians as an "arrangement," or, more informally, a "roadmap." The roadmap for the performance of "Now's the Time" might be something as simple—and general, since it can be used to describe countless jazz performances—as "Intro – Head – Sax Solo – Trumpet Solo – Head." This roadmap leaves out the section immediately following the trumpet solo, which almost sounds like a mistake: perhaps Davis ended his solo one chorus early, leaving Parker unprepared to come back in with the head; perhaps he expected his solo to be followed by a piano solo, but Dizzy Gillespie (who happened to be playing the piano on this recording) declined, the piano not being his main instrument. Even if it was a mistake, the continuous playing of the rhythm section holds the performance together, keeping the rhythm and harmony going until the horns enter with the return of the head.

In contrast to the "arrangement" or "roadmap," jazz musicians use the word "form" to describe the structure of one chorus of the tune being played. In *What to Listen for in Jazz*, Barry Kernfeld calls this structure "chorus form" and defines it as "a sequence of chords tied to a metric scheme."[3] Thus, according to Kernfeld, the form of "Now's the Time" consists of not only the harmonic progression, but also the twelve-measure length of one chorus. I would like to modify Kernfeld's definition, and define a tune's form as consisting of the harmonic progression in conjunction with its phrase structure. With my definition, the form of "Now's the Time" (as well as its structurally and harmonically equivalent surrogate "Knows the Thyme"[4]) is that of the specific manifestation of the twelve-bar blues notated as a lead sheet in figure 3.2: the form, that is, consists of not only

Figure 3.2.   Lead sheet for "Knows the Thyme."

a common blues harmonic progression, but also the organization of this progression into three four-measure phrases. The difference between my definition and Kernfeld's is a subtle but crucial one; it will allow us to consider the ways that a musician's improvisation can be affected not only by the harmonic progression and the length of the chorus, but also by the internal phrase organization of that chorus. Furthermore, we will see in the analyses later in this chapter that the specific quality created by the melody and harmonic progression of each phrase can also factor into a musician's performance; the quality of a phrase's "feel"—where the phrase moves forward, where it relaxes, where it feels static, etc.—often carries over into an improvisation, even though the composed melody has been temporarily set aside.

Turnarounds and Breaks

As previously described, jazz musicians typically create a performance by stringing together several choruses, or repetitions of a tune's form. Kernfeld describes a feature common to most of the forms that jazz musicians use, a feature that allows for the repetition of the form. He writes:

> [There is] a lack of coincidence between points of arrival—the cadence on the tonic chord, which falls 2 (sometimes 4) bars before the end of a chorus, and the strongest metric downbeat, which falls on the first bar of the next chorus. The result is a formal instability that perpetually energizes a piece, pushing it toward a simultaneous resolution of harmony and rhythm but never allowing it to reach that resolution.[5]

In other words, a strong metric—or structural—downbeat occurs each time the form repeats, and this downbeat is at odds with, and conflicts with, the feeling of arrival upon reaching the final tonic. Figure 3.3 graphs a portion of a performance of "Now's the Time," showing this gap between the point of harmonic arrival and the structural downbeat. Here, the harmonic progression resolves to the tonic F^7 in m. 11; the feeling of arrival (and closure) on this chord is enhanced by the forward-moving dominant progressions that strongly lead to it. The arrows below the staff combine to describe the metric and phrase structure of the chorus. Both the melody and the harmonic

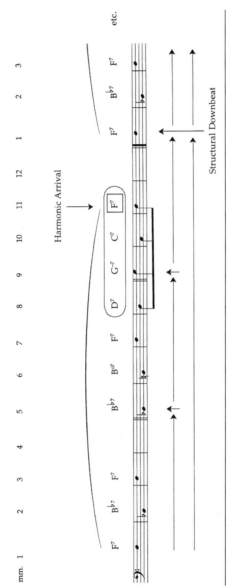

Figure 3.3. Gap between point of harmonic arrival and structural downbeat.

progression contribute to the definition of four-measure phrases. The melody begins with a pick-up to m. 1, and continues to beat 3 of m. 4; it then repeats (with only slight modification) beginning with a pick-up into m. 5, continuing into m. 8; the final phrase introduces new material, and begins with a pick-up into m. 9, before coming to a close in m. 11. The harmonic progression also contributes to this phrase structure by returning to the tonic F^7 in the third measure of each phrase, creating a sense of closure: the first part of each phrase introduces tension by either moving away from tonic or beginning on a chord other than tonic, and this tension is then resolved in the third measure when the progression returns to the tonic. These melodic and harmonic characteristics contribute to a strong sense of four-measure phrases, creating a predictable, metric accent at the beginning of each phrase, that is, in mm. 1, 5, and 9 of each chorus. Similarly, the repetition of the entire form creates an even stronger sense of a "structural downbeat" at the point that the form "starts over."

Kernfeld says that the gap created between the point of harmonic arrival and the structural downbeat creates a feeling of energy, and the resulting formal instability pushes the music forward into the next chorus. A common way that musicians take advantage of this gap and resulting forward motion is with the performance practice known as a "break." A break is usually used to set up an individual musician's solo, and is created when the rhythm section stops abruptly on the downbeat of the measure containing the first point of arrival—that is, the point two or four measures before the end of the chorus where the harmonic progression comes to rest on the tonic. The rhythm section then remains silent until the structural downbeat at the beginning of the next chorus. Thus, the break creates an abrupt rift in the texture, which the soloist usually fills with an improvised line that rushes forward, leading to the beginning of the next chorus, where the rhythm section then re-enters. Figure 3.4 is a transcription of a famous break from the recording of the Clifford Brown/Max Roach Quintet's performance of "Cherokee."[6] The example begins four measures before the end of the first chorus statement of the head. Two measures before the end of the chorus, at the arrival on a B♭ tonic, the rhythm section cuts off abruptly, creating a break, which trumpeter Clifford Brown fills with a very fast, exciting, forward-moving line

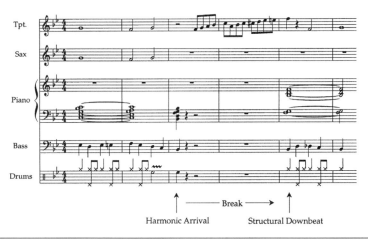

Figure 3.4. Clifford Brown, "Cherokee," break between head and solo.

that slingshots the performance into the next chorus. The rhythm section then comes back in, riding the wave of excitement generated by the break. Clifford's break not only propels the music forward, but also sets the tone for his exciting, energetic solo that follows.

Another common way that musicians link these two points of arrival is through the use of a "turnaround." A turnaround is a series of harmonies that begins immediately after the final tonic of the form and leads strongly to the beginning of the next repetition of the form. Since the goal of a turnaround is literally to turn the music around—that is, to lead back to the top of the form—it is typically constructed by combining a series of harmonies generated through goal-oriented dominant or tritone substitution functions. Figure 3.5a demonstrates one of the most common turnarounds, inserted into the last two measures of "Knows the Thyme." After arriving at the tonic F^7 in m. 11, the harmonic progression sets up the next repetition of the form by stringing together dominant functions, leading from D^7 through G^{-7} to C^7, which then moves to F^7 on the metrically accented first measure of the next chorus. Some other common turnarounds are illustrated in figure 3.5b–d. In figure 3.5b, the penultimate harmony—C^7, which leads strongly to the following F^7 through a dominant function—is preceded by two chords derived through the tritone-substitution function. The turnaround in figure 3.5c generates all of its harmonies through the tritone-substitution function, with $A\flat^7$ sliding down to G^7, which

a. Turnaround inserted into final two measures of "Knows the Thyme."

b.

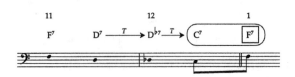

c.

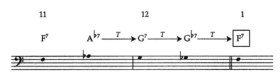

d.

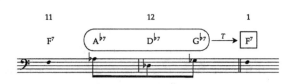

Figure 3.5.   Turnarounds.

slides down to G♭⁷, which in turn slides down to F⁷ at the beginning of the next chorus. The final turnaround, notated in figure 3.5d, again combines dominant and tritone-substitution functions. Working backwards, the penultimate G♭⁷, which leads to the F⁷ through the tritone-substitution function, is preceded by two harmonies generated through the dominant function, namely, A♭⁷ and D♭⁷.

By combining the strongly goal-oriented, dominant and tritone-substitution progressions with an increase in the rate of harmonic rhythm, these turnarounds, like the break, serve to propel the

Figure 3.6.   John Coltrane, "Blues by Five," turnaround, mm. 11–12.

music forward into the next chorus. A soloist will often respond to a turnaround's increased harmonic activity by improvising a forward moving line that weaves in and around these harmonies, as can be seen in figure 3.6, which is from John Coltrane's solo on "Blues by Five."[7] In this example, Coltrane's melody strongly defines the underlying harmony: the introduction of B♮ on beat 3 of the first measure implies G^7; this note resolves to C, the root of C^{-7}, on beat 2 of the following measure; and the final portion leads from the root of F^7 on beat 3 of this measure to the root of B♭^{7} on the downbeat of the first measure of the next chorus. Coltrane contributes to the sense of forward motion by emphasizing the pitches of the underlying goal-oriented harmonic progression, but also by improvising a melody that always leads somewhere; rather than treating each chord as a springboard, reacting to each one as it occurs, Coltrane takes an active role, *guiding* the harmonic progression, improvising a melody that leads to G^7, then C^{-7}, and, finally into the B♭^{7} that begins the next chorus.

Common Forms

The jazz repertoire consists of hundreds if not thousands of tunes, and learning to negotiate this huge repertoire is one of the most important skills a jazz musician must acquire. His or her job is made easier in that most jazz tunes fall into one of two formal categories: blues forms and song forms. While melodies and harmonic progressions vary from tune to tune, an understanding of the phrase structures of these two forms combined with a knowledge of common harmonic progressions helps a musician deal with this large corpus.

Like "Now's the Time," most blues forms are twelve measures long and break down into three four-measure phrases. As described in the previous chapter, there isn't just one harmonic progression for the blues, but rather a large number of related progressions. There are likewise different possibilities for a blues tune's phrase structure. In the case of

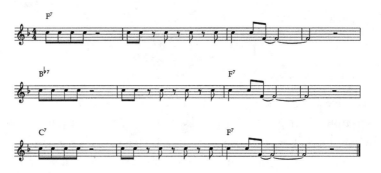

Figure 3.7.   "F Jam Blues."

Figure 3.8.   "Blues for Ellis."

"Now's the Time," the phrase structure could be described as AAB; the first A phrase (mm. 1–4) is repeated (mm. 5–8), and the final B phrase (mm. 9–12) contrasts with the two As. This is probably the most common blues-form phrase structure, and is most likely influenced by the lyrics of classic blues tunes, many of which follow this AAB prototype.

Figures 3.7 and 3.8 show two more possible blues forms, one simpler and one more complex than "Knows the Thyme"/"Now's the Time." The composition "F Jam Blues" (comparable to Duke Ellington's "C Jam Blues") notated in figure 3.7, is a model of simplicity; not only is the melody made up of only two different pitches, but each four-measure phrase is exactly the same, yielding a phrase structure of AAA. The harmony is also pared down to the bare minimum needed for it to be recognized as a blues progression; this progression was described in chapter 2 as the "deep structure" of the blues progression. This tune's title is appropriate, as its simplicity makes it perfect for informal, nonrehearsed performances, or "jam sessions."

Figure 3.9. "Footsteps."

The composition "Blues for Ellis," notated in figure 3.8 (comparable to Charlie Parker's "Blues for Alice"), contrasts with both "F Jam Blues" and "Knows the Thyme" by greatly increasing the complexity of both the harmonic progression and the phrase structure. Here, the melody spins out over the course of the entire form, winding through and around the colorful harmonic progression, never repeating itself, and therefore not setting up a predictable, repetitive phrase structure.

Blues tunes need not be twelve measures long, however. Figure 3.9 is a lead sheet for a composition titled "Footsteps" (which is similar to Wayne Shorter's composition "Footprints"). This tune modifies the blues form in interesting ways. First, the length of the form is twice as long as the standard twelve-bar blues, although the form still breaks into three phrases, with this tune's eight-measure phrases also being twice as long as the four-measure phrases of the standard blues. The typical blues harmonic progression has also been transformed; a standard blues is based on dominant-seventh harmonies, while this blues is based on minor-seventh harmonies. Musicians refer to blues tunes with this kind of harmony as "minor" blues.

Figure 3.10 shows that while the modality of the tune has been changed, the harmonies themselves can still be derived from the

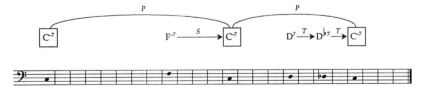

Figure 3.10. "Footsteps," analysis of harmonic progression.

blues' deep structure defined in chapter 2. The first phrase (mm. 1–8) prolongs the tonic C^{-7}, the F^{-7} of the second phrase (mm. 9–16) returns to the tonic through the subdominant function, and D^7 and D♭^{7} move strongly to the tonic through dominant-derived tritone-substitution functions. By preserving the phrase structure and basic harmonic identity of the standard twelve-bar blues, this tune is still recognizable as a blues, despite its transformation.

In addition to the blues, another very common form used in jazz is the "thirty-two-bar song form." Virtually all thirty-two-bar song forms break into four eight-measure phrases, and although the pattern of repetition and contrast between the phrases may vary from tune to tune, certain phrase structures are more common than others. The tune "Rhythm-A-Ning," which has its harmonic progression and phrase structure notated in figure 3.11, provides an example of the most common thirty-two-bar phrase structure, which can be described as AABA.[8] The first A phrase (mm. 1–8) is repeated (mm. 9–16), then followed by a contrasting phrase—the bridge, or B section, mm. 17–24—which is in turn followed by a return of the initial A phrase in mm. 25–32.

Another common thirty-two-bar phrase structure is demonstrated in figure 3.12, which contains the harmonic progression and phrase structure for "How High the Moon." The phrase structure of this tune might be described as ABAB: the first A phrase (mm. 1–8) is constructed from a melodic and harmonic sequence and is followed by a contrasting B phrase (mm. 9–16). Halfway through the tune, in m. 17, the A phrase returns, followed by a repetition of the B phrase modified slightly to allow for a sense of closure by returning to the final G major tonic.

While both "Rhythm-A-Ning" and "How High the Moon" are thirty-two-bar song forms, their specific phrase structures give each its own "feel," and much of this difference in feel has to do with the way the tunes structure the flow of time through the use—and reuse—of thematic material and harmonic progressions. In "How High the Moon," the first half (mm. 1–16) ends by leaving the listener hanging; the harmonic progression ends with a half cadence on D^7, and the melody ends by repeating the pitch D, the dominant of the overall key of G major. The tension created by this lack of closure dissipates

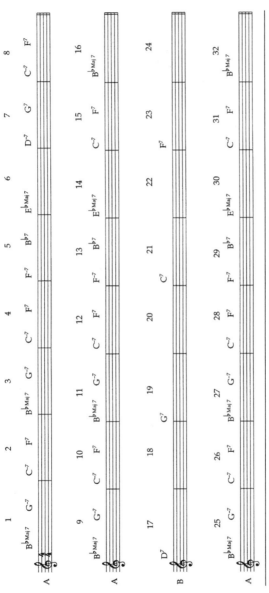

Figure 3.11. Harmonic progression and phrase structure for "Rhythm-A-Ning" (Thelonious Monk).

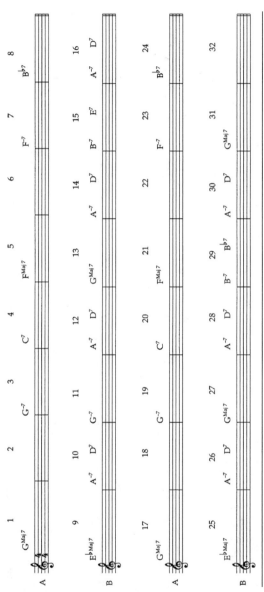

Figure 3.12.   Harmonic progression and phrase structure for "How High the Moon" (Lewis/Hamilton).

in m. 17 with the return of the opening material and the accompanying harmonic motion to the tonic G^{Maj7} chord. The harmonic progression and thematic material of "Rhythm-A-Ning," on the other hand, creates a very different feeling. Whereas "How High the Moon" ended its first half by creating harmonic and melodic tension that is only resolved by the return of the opening material at the beginning of its second half, "Rhythm-A-Ning" instead creates a strong sense of closure in m. 16—also the end of its first half—by moving to the tonic harmony through a series of dominant progressions. Also in contrast to the release of tension "How High the Moon" creates in m. 17 by returning to the opening melody and tonic harmony, "Rhythm-A-Ning" creates a heightened sense of tension at the beginning of its second half by introducing both new thematic material and the non-diatonic harmony D^7. This section also creates a strong sense of forward motion by stringing together dominant functions in a large-scale, extended progression that leads all the way across the structural boundary into the final A section's return of the opening material and tonic B♭^{Maj7} in m. 25.

The different "feels" created by specific phrase structures can have a strong effect on the way that musicians improvise over these forms, as we can see in figure 3.13, which is Charlie Rouse's first improvised chorus on "Rhythm-A-Ning."[9] In this improvisation, Rouse conveys the feel of the composition's phrase structure; throughout the first section, he improvises relatively short, segmented phrases that not only do not flow across the structural boundaries that separate the primary eight-measure phrases, but also segment these sections into strongly defined two- and four-measure phrases, as shown by the slurs in the example. Again, conforming to the underlying phrase structure, Rouse wraps things up at the end of the first half in m. 16 by rounding off his phrase, coming to a close on the tonic pitch B♭. In the B section (mm. 17–24), however, his improvisation takes on a different character; after his initial opening gesture in mm. 17–18, he begins a long phrase that flows from m. 19 across the four-measure subphrase boundary in m. 21 before ending at the end of m. 22. By improvising across this boundary, Rouse counteracts the sense of segmentation he had created in his A sections, creating more of a feeling of flow and forward motion. With his next phrase, Rouse continues this forward motion by improvising across the structural boundary into the following A section in

Figure 3.13. Charlie Rouse, "Rhythm-A-Ning," saxophone solo, mm. 1–32.

m. 25. Rouse again avoids improvising across the structural boundary at the end of this final A section, creating a sense of closure by ending his line on the tonic Bb in m. 31.

To summarize the effect of the tune's phrase structure on his improvisation, Rouse's A section improvisations seem self-contained; he rounds off the phrase at the end of each A section before beginning the next section. It's as if he inhabits these sections without a thought of what is coming ahead or what has come before. His improvisation on the bridge, on the other hand, sounds unsettled and forward looking, as if the tension created by the introduction of the new material as well as the long, goal-oriented harmonic progression leading into the final A section had a direct effect on his improvisation.

Keeping the Form

By knowing and understanding a tune's form, jazz musicians are able to coordinate their improvised group performances. Because the form of a tune is what keeps each musician in the right place at the right time, musicians place a strong emphasis on "keeping the form," that is, on making one's improvisation consistently and accurately conform to a tune's harmonic progression and phrase structure. Since a jazz performance generally consists of many repetitions of a tune's form—in the playing of the head at the beginning and end, and through each of the improvised solos—a given tune's form often becomes second nature to a musician, and musicians are often judged on their ability to "keep the form."

While the ability to keep the form can be used to separate the experienced from the less-experienced musician, this is not to say that professional musicians never "lose the form." In fact, sometimes they lose it to magical effect. On his famous recording of "Misterioso," which is transcribed in figure 3.14, Thelonious Monk inserts an extra measure into his two-chorus blues solo.[10] Monk keeps the form through his first chorus, but at the beginning of the second chorus, he seems to lose his place.

Figure 3.15 shows how Monk's improvisation is exactly one measure out of phase with the harmonic progression, which is clearly

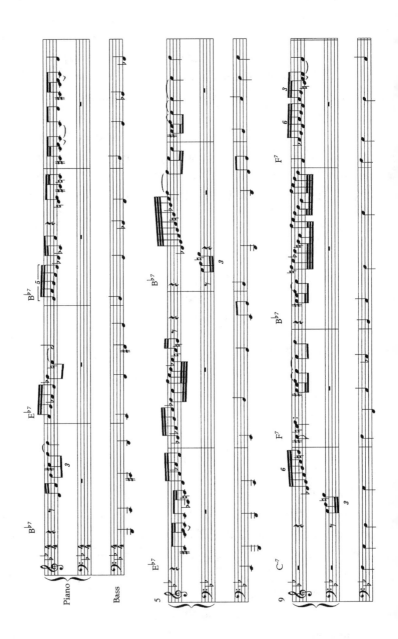

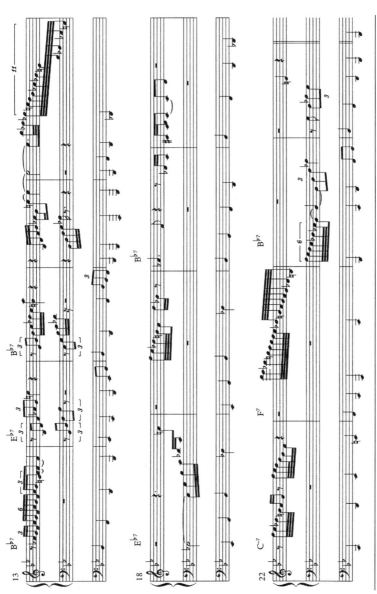

Figure 3.14.   Thelonious Monk, "Misterioso," piano solo, mm. 1–24.

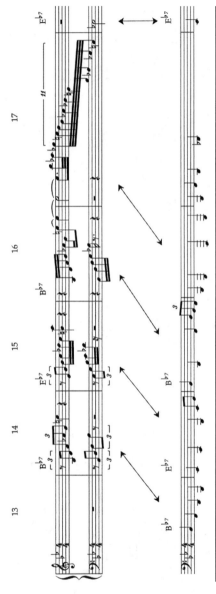

Figure 3.15.   Thelonious Monk, "Misterioso," piano solo, mm. 13–17. *Pianist and bassist out of phase.*

defined by bassist John Simmons. While Monk does briefly lose the form in this phrase, Simmons hears what's happening and modifies his bass line to accommodate the expanded first phrase by waiting an extra measure before moving to $E\flat^7$. By the time he reaches the fourth measure of this second chorus (m. 16), Monk also seems to realize that something is wrong, and when he reaches the long (over four beats!) high $E\natural$, it sounds as if he stops to get his bearings before playing a descending whole-tone scale to signal the move to $E\flat^7$. Interestingly, his solo up to this point has been so dissonant that the clashes created by being out of phase with the harmonic progression do not really sound like mistakes, but like more of the same.[11] This example points out that while the ability to keep the form is important, it is even more important for each musician to listen to the other members of the ensemble in order to adapt his or her performance to account for any formal anomalies that may arise in the course of a performance.

While a tune's form has a strong control over each musician in a small jazz group performance and this control allows the musicians to coordinate their improvisations, each musician has a range of possibilities for relating their individual improvisations to the form. The soloist may improvise a line that either conforms to a tune's phrase structure or de-emphasizes it by overlapping its formal boundaries. Similarly, the soloist may "run the changes"—that is, play a line that explicitly defines and conforms to the harmonic progression of the tune—or may improvise a melody that more loosely defines the harmony. Like the soloist, the members of the rhythm section may also weakly or strongly define either the harmonic progression or the phrase structure of the tune while still keeping the form. In chapter 2, we saw how the rhythm section coordinates to present the harmonic progression, and in a similar way, they also coordinate to define a tune's phrase structure. Among the five common types of interaction listed in his article "Preliminary Thoughts on Analyzing Interaction Among Jazz Performers," Paul Rinzler describes how the musicians may interact by "accenting the end of formal units."

> There are two main formal units that may be accented: an entire chorus, or a phrase (most often a four- or eight-bar phrase). There is a very strong tendency for both the soloist and the rhythm section to highlight

in some manner the end of a formal unit and the beginning of the next. The soloist has the option, often a favored one, to end or begin phrases in the improvised melody line at the end of a formal unit. The rhythm section has a similarly favored option either to fill during the break in the soloist's phrasing at the end of a formal unit or to accent the end of the formal unit even if the soloist is continuing a phrase.[12]

Rinzler's description, while accurate for some performances, oversimplifies—and overgeneralizes—this process. By designating the process of accenting the end of formal units as "favored," he seems to prescribe jazz performances in which the musicians predictably and unambiguously parse out the music in even four- or eight-measure chunks, ignoring many individual performances and more general styles of jazz that value the blurring of formal boundaries. In the analyses later in this chapter, we will see examples of performances that strongly define formal boundaries as well as performances that blur those boundaries.

In *Thinking in Jazz*, Paul Berliner presents a more carefully nuanced description of the flexibility of this process by discussing different ways rhythm section members can define a tune's phrase structure through the use of "structural markers." He considers each member of the rhythm section in turn, first describing bassists:

> They may consistently bring the character of certain chords within the progression into clear profile as structural markers, whereas they take great liberties in the interpretation of other chords. Players may introduce emphatic markers in varying degrees of density in different parts of the form. Some may emphasize root and fifth playing on the first chord of major harmonic segments; others may feature this approach whenever chords change. Still others may favor, generally, a greater emphasis on 'outside' harmonic invention than on 'inside' playing.[13]

He similarly describes the range of possibilities for drummers:

> Drummers may also interpret and represent the music's structure at various levels of organization. To mark the boundaries between four-measure segments of a progression, they can maintain a time-keeping pattern for three measures . . . then increase the rhythmic density in the fourth measure. They resolve its tension by returning to the

time-keeping pattern in the fifth measure, sometimes emphasizing the return with a definitive accent on the downbeat or the second half of the preceding beat. Towards such ends, drummers commonly perform specialized one- or two-bar fills as structural markers. . . .

To delineate larger harmonic components, a player can apply the same procedure over the eighth and ninth bars, or the sixteenth and seventeenth bars, or, to signal the close of each chorus, the last few measures of the form. Drummers may reserve the use of particular figures, such as press rolls, for the last turnaround of a solo, marking off the larger performance. (328)

Although he describes these ways that drummers can emphasize structural markers, he also says that while one drummer might explicitly mark the form, "another takes great liberties in interpreting rhythmic form, obscuring the metric structure to create suspense" (329). We will see examples of both kinds of drumming later in the chapter in the analyses of "Blues by Five" and "E.S.P."

Finally, Berliner turns to pianists, saying that they have the option of "delineating the form at different structural levels." He goes on to describe some of the possible ways a pianist can do this:

To portray large structural units, pianists can punctuate the music rhythmically with block chords over an A section, then create a contrasting texture by improvising sweeping free-rhythm arpeggios over the B section, thus floating the time. In subtler terms, they can outline short structural units by repeating a crisply articulated off-beat pattern over the course of four-measure progressions, then resolve the pattern's tension with a chord on the downbeat of the fifth (335).

Again, unlike Rinzler, Berliner goes on to say that these are only possibilities, and that different pianists playing in different styles may either emphasize or blur the phrase structure:

Some pianists are generally less concerned with explicit time-keeping aspects of their role and may consequently minimize or abandon the performance of repeating structural markers. They are more concerned, rather, with developing, according to their own internal logic, original ideas that occur to them, or developing ideas that emerge from the collective conversational aspects of improvisation (335).

Again, we will see examples of both of these different approaches in the analyses later in the chapter.

Not only may the rhythm section members coordinate and interact to define a tune's form, but there is also the potential for interaction between the soloist and the rhythm section. As described above, both the rhythm section and the soloist may strongly emphasize the phrase structure, strongly demarcating formal divisions. Each may also de-emphasize the phrase structure in favor of creating longer melodic lines and harmonic textures that overlap these phrases—in a sense, playing the harmonic progression more than the phrase structure. Furthermore, the rhythm section's and the soloist's choice to emphasize or de-emphasize the phrase structure may be based on what the other is doing. For example, if the soloist is strongly defining the form, the rhythm section may (1) follow the soloist's lead and further reinforce the form by emphasizing the boundaries of formal units, or (2) relax into a more neutral definition of the phrase structure to balance out the soloist's emphasis on the form. Similarly, if a soloist's improvisation de-emphasizes a tune's form, the rhythm section may respond by (3) strongly emphasizing the form in order to provide a solid background against which the soloist's explorations can be heard and understood, or (4) "go along for the ride" and blur the formal boundaries along with the soloist, creating a performance that feels more liquid and less parsed into even, predictable, four- or eight-measure time spans. The following analyses examine performances in which the musicians, while still "keeping the form," approach the process of defining the form in different ways.

"Blues by Five": Balancing Formal Definition

Figure 3.16 is the lead sheet for the Red Garland composition "Blues by Five," recorded by the "classic" Miles Davis Quintet on the album *Cookin'*.[14] This quintet consisted of trumpeter Miles Davis, saxophonist John Coltrane, pianist Red Garland, bassist Paul Chambers, and drummer Philly Joe Jones, and is considered a good example of a group that plays in the *hard bop* style. By examining the lead sheet, we can see that the form of "Blues by Five" is a good example of a twelve-bar blues:

Figure 3.16. "Blues by Five" (Red Garland). (© 1965 Prestige Music (BMI). Copyright renewed. Courtesy of Prestige Music, a div. of Concord Music Group, Inc. All Rights Reserved. Used by Permission.)

not only is the harmonic progression common—it's the one defined in the previous chapter as the "Jazz" blues progression—but the phrase structure parses neatly into three four-measure phrases. Within each of these phrases, the melody follows a predictable pattern: it begins with a quarter-note pick-up to the first measure of the phrase; extends to the end of either m. 3 (in the first two phrases) or m. 2 (in the third phrase); and is then followed by a rest that both defines the ending of one phrase and sets up the beginning of the next. This lead sheet presents the raw material on which the musicians base their improvisations; an aspect of jazz musicians' personal styles is the amount of control they let the tune exert over their improvisations—how closely they follow the tune's harmonic progression and phrase structure.

In this performance, which is a head arrangement, Davis takes the first solo, and the first three choruses of his solo are transcribed in figure 3.17a. Throughout these choruses, Davis follows the tune's phrase structure very closely: his phrases almost always begin on or near the downbeat of the phrase's first measure and end in the third measure, after which they are followed by a rest until the next phrase begins. If we compare this improvisation with Coltrane's, which immediately follows Davis's in the performance, we see that Coltrane takes a very different approach toward improvising on this form. Figure 3.17b is a transcription of the first three choruses of Coltrane's solo. In contrast to Davis, Coltrane improvises phrases that rarely coincide with the even four-measure phrase structure of the tune. On

Figure 3.17a. Miles Davis, "Blues by Five," trumpet solo, mm. 1–36.

the contrary, Coltrane usually begins somewhere in the middle of the phrases defined by the form, often in the second or third measure, and continues over the structural boundaries, ending in the first or second measure of the next phrase. Another difference between Davis's and Coltrane's improvised phrases has to do with the consistency of the phrases' lengths. By sticking closely to the tune's phrase structure, Davis generally improvises melodies that are approximately three measures long, which he follows with one measure of rest, resulting in a string of four-measure phrases. Coltrane's improvised melodies, on the other hand, are more irregular. For example, his first phrase is three measures long, followed by a measure of rest; his second phrase

Figure 3.17b.   John Coltrane, "Blues by Five," saxophone solo, mm. 1–36.

is only one measure long, and is followed by two measures of rest; his third phrase is just over four measures long, and is followed by almost two measures of rest, and so on.

Figure 3.18 graphically charts the differences between the way that Davis's and Coltrane's phrases relate to the phrase structure of the tune. The series of vertical lines along the horizontal axis at the top designate a metric hierarchy: each line marks off a measure; the thicker lines mark off each four-measure phrase; and the thickest lines mark the boundaries of each twelve-measure chorus. Line *a* maps the melody of "Blues by Five" onto this axis; the thick horizontal lines show where each phrase begins and ends, as well as the amount of

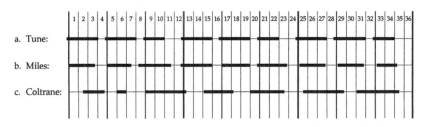

Figure 3.18.   Graphic comparison of tune and solos, "Blues by Five."

space between each phrase. Line *b* similarly graphs the first three improvised choruses of Davis's solo, and the similarity between the phrase structure of Davis's solo and the original melody is very easy to see. Coltrane's solo is graphed in line *c*, and it is also easy to see that, unlike Davis's, his improvisation does not conform to the phrase structure of the head, but rather takes a much freer approach. The musical effect of the contrasting styles is interesting: Davis's simple, melodic phrases contrast nicely with Coltrane's more complex, florid lines; likewise, Davis's regular, four-measure phrases sound more grounded, logical, and inevitable, while Coltrane's irregular phrases sound more like a spontaneous stream of consciousness.

Examining the way the rhythm section supports and interacts with these two different improvisational styles yields interesting results. Figure 3.19 is a full transcription of the piano, bass, and drum parts for Davis's first improvised chorus. Red Garland's piano comping is light, sparse, and conversational, filling in the gaps in Davis's solo. While he does play within the form of the tune, Garland doesn't explicitly emphasize any structural markers until the end of the chorus, where his increased activity and more aggressive touch signals a significant formal boundary. Paul Chambers's walking bass line also follows the form, but his undifferentiated string of quarter-notes doesn't actually do anything to explicitly define the four-measure structural phrases. Philly Joe Jones's drum part consists primarily of time-keeping patterns on the ride cymbal and hi-hat, with occasional syncopated hits on the snare drum. At the end of the first four-measure phrase, he subtly marks the structural boundary by ever-so-slightly increasing his rhythmic activity. After this, he doesn't do anything to mark the boundary between the end of the second phrase and the beginning of the third phrase, but he does strongly mark the structural boundary at the end of the chorus by

Figure 3.19. Miles Davis, "Blues by Five," trumpet solo, mm. 1–12.

playing a strong rhythmic pattern on the snare and bass drums. Taken together, the rhythm section does "keep the form," albeit rather loosely; they keep the time and define the harmony, but do not strongly mark the boundaries of the four-measure structural phrases.

During Coltrane's solo, on the other hand, the rhythm section behaves very differently. From the start of the solo, each member increases their rhythmic activity, especially near the end of each

Figure 3.20. John Coltrane, "Blues by Five," saxophone solo, third chorus.

four-measure structural phrase. By the time Coltrane reaches his fourth chorus, transcribed in full in figure 3.20, Garland and Jones have synchronized their parts: Garland begins to repeat a four-measure pattern over and over, and Jones "locks-up" with this pattern with his snare and bass drums. This locking-up has two immediate effects: (1) the increased intensity caused by the interaction and coordination between the players boosts the energy level of the performance; and

Figure 3.21. "Blues by Five," saxophone solo, third chorus, piano and drum parts.

(2) because the pattern is four measures long and has most of its activity in its fourth measure, it very strongly marks the structural boundaries of each four-measure phrase.

Figure 3.21 isolates the piano and drum parts for this chorus, allowing us to more closely examine this synchronization. For the first three measures of each four-measure phrase, Garland and Jones anticipate the downbeat, playing on the "and" of the fourth beat of the previous measure. This syncopated anticipation creates a very strong sense of forward motion, propelling the music into the next measure; it's almost as if the music is moving forward so strongly that the next measure arrives a half of a beat early. This effect is enhanced by the fact that Garland not only rhythmically anticipates the downbeat of the following measure, but anticipates the harmony as well: immediately before the downbeat of the first measure he plays a voicing of a B♭⁷ (identifiable because of its inclusion of that chord's 3rd and 7th); immediately before the downbeat of the second measure he anticipates the change to E♭⁷; similarly, he anticipates the third measure's return to B♭⁷ at the end of m. 2; and so on. Garland and Jones punctuate the end of each phrase with a longer rhythmic pattern that Jones sets up with two quick sixteenth notes on the snare drum. These faster rhythmic values propel the musicians into the closing gesture, which marks the structural boundary between the four-measure phrases in an interesting way. Up to this point, Jones and Garland have played on upbeats only, but at this point, they land squarely on beat 2 before playing a dotted quarter-note on beat 3. By landing on the beat rather than anticipating it, they resolve some of the tension and instability they created earlier in the phrase. Furthermore, by sustaining the dotted quarter-note on beat 3 they create a feeling of temporal suspension; it's almost as if the time is stretched out like a rubber band, which then snaps back when the musicians play the accented chord voicing and bass drum hit on the "and" of beat 4, simultaneously finishing the first phrase as well as setting up the next.

These examples demonstrate that when accompanying two very different soloists, this rhythm section responds in very different ways. Behind Davis, the rhythm section weakly defines the phrase structure, whereas behind Coltrane they strongly define it. Furthermore, the way that the rhythm section treats the phrase structure seems to be in response to the soloist: since Davis's improvisation strongly defines the tune's phrase structure, the rhythm section doesn't need to; likewise, when the rhythm section hears that Coltrane is obscuring the tune's form by playing over and through its structural boundaries, they respond by strongly emphasizing these boundaries, and in the process create a strong background for Coltrane to play off of. Thus, in this particular performance, the musicians engage in a balancing act; there seems to be a general agreement that the form should be clearly defined, but the task of defining it is not assigned to any particular musician or group of musicians. Rather, it is a group effort, negotiated in the course of the performance. Because the form is clearly defined by either the soloist or the rhythm section throughout this performance, a listener has an easy time following along and keeping track of the form. This balancing, or sharing, of the task of formal definition between the musicians is characteristic of certain styles of jazz (including *hard bop*), but not of others, as we will see in the next analysis.

"E.S.P.": Going with the Flow

In the mid-1960s, Miles Davis formed another group that has become known as his "Second Great Quintet." Besides Davis, this group included saxophonist Wayne Shorter, pianist Herbie Hancock, bassist Ron Carter, and drummer Tony Williams. The music created by this quintet contrasts in a number of ways with that of the "classic" quintet of the mid-1950s. An obvious contrast between these groups is the choice of repertoire: while the '50s quintet tended to play blues like "Blues by Five" and standards like "If I Were a Bell" or "My Funny Valentine," the '60s quintet tended to perform original compositions by the group's members. The two groups also contrast in the way that the rhythm section members fulfill their roles in the ensemble. Each member of the '50s quintet's rhythm section was fairly consistent in their approach: the bassist would almost always walk, the drummer would almost always play repetitive rhythms on the ride pattern and hi-hat, and the pianist would almost always comp with short, light, syncopated chords. The rhythm section of the '60s quintet, on the other hand, took a freer approach: drummer Tony Williams constantly varied his time-keeping patterns, bassist Ron Carter made more use of ostinati and pedal tones as well as walking bass lines, and pianist Herbie Hancock's comping was much more intricate, complex, and contrapuntal. A final contrast has to do with the way that these groups define the form of a tune in the course of a performance. As we saw in the previous section, the members of the '50s quintet shared the process of defining the form; either the soloist or the rhythm section tended to emphasize the structural boundaries of the tune's phrases. As we will see in the following analysis, the '60s quintet tended to blur these boundaries, creating performances that sound more fluid and less structured.

The album *E.S.P.* was the first of six studio albums recorded by the '60s group; figure 3.22 notates the harmonic progression, phrase structure, and opening melodic motive for the title tune.[15] This tune, which is representative of the type of repertoire played by the '60s quintet, sounds very different from the kinds of tunes performed by the '50s quintet. A number of factors contribute to this difference. First, the kinds of harmonies used are much more colorful and complex than simple 7th chords. The first harmony, E^{7alt}, is a good example. The first two notes of the melody—C($\flat$13) and G($\sharp$9)—clash colorfully with the underlying E^7, transforming it from a simple E^7 to E^{7alt}. Most of the other harmonies in this piece are similarly transformed. Because the melody throughout is made up primarily of colorful, dissonant, upper harmonic extensions, it creates a feeling of detachment, as if it floats over the harmony, rather than being bound by it.

The way that the chords progress in this piece is also very different from that of the blues and standards of the earlier repertoire. Gone are the goal-oriented, teleological progressions of function-derived harmonies, and in their place are vacillating progressions that ambiguously slide around, primarily shifting up or down by semitone or tone. By combining dissonant, colorful harmonies in ambiguous, non-function-derived progressions, this tune tends to negate any feeling of arrival, creating a circular, free-flowing, nonsegmented feeling. Harmonic ambiguity and melodic detachment notwithstanding, this piece does still conform to a common thirty-two-bar ABAB form, with some demarcation of the phrase structure evident. The identical first and third eight-measure phrases contrast with the second and fourth phrases both harmonically and melodically. In the first and third phrases, the chords last two measures each, wandering up and down by semitone: E – F – E – E$\flat$. In the second (and fourth) phrase, the harmonic rhythm accelerates—the chords last only one measure, rather than two—and a larger, more extended harmonic motion takes place: D ascends to E$\flat$, which continues ascending through E, finally arriving at F. The melody of the second phrase (not notated here) also contrasts with that of the first, creating a broader contour compared to the repetitive melodic zigzags of the first phrase. Nevertheless, without the feeling of arrival created by goal-oriented harmonic progressions

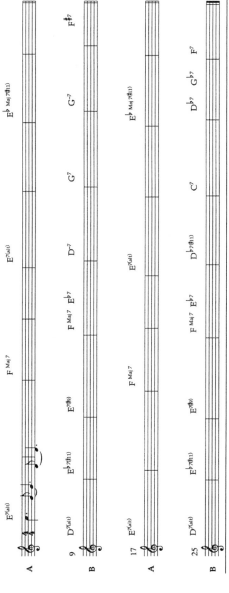

Figure 3.22. Harmonic progression, phrase structure, and opening motive for "E.S.P." (Wayne Shorter).

and melodies, the form of this tune still feels somewhat freer and less clearly demarcated than that of the '50s repertoire.

Throughout the performance of this tune, the soloists tend to respond to this somewhat ambiguous tune by improvising lines that further blur its formal boundaries, and we will see that the rhythm section tends to "go with the flow" created by the soloist; that is, they often play accompaniment patterns that support this blurring of the phrase structure, rather than try to balance out the improvisation's formal ambiguity by emphasizing structural markers, as in the previous analysis. We can hear an example of this in the final chorus of Wayne Shorter's saxophone solo, transcribed in figure 3.23.[16]

In figure 3.24, which graphically charts this improvised chorus, we can see that Shorter's phrases rarely align with the tune's phrase structure: line *a* lays out the tune's predictable pattern of four eight-measure phrases as a timeline, while line *b* maps Shorter's improvised phrases onto this axis. Like Coltrane on "Blues by Five," Shorter is not constrained by the tune's phrase structure, but instead tends to improvise across these boundaries. Here, he begins with a four-measure phrase (mm. 1–4), which he follows with an eight-measure phrase (mm. 5–12) that extends across the tune's first A-B structural boundary. This is followed by a five-measure phrase (mm. 13–17), which in turn is followed by a seven-measure phrase (mm. 18–24). At this point, Shorter's solo realigns with the tune's phrase structure, and he rounds out his improvisation with a nine-measure phrase that begins with a pick-up into m. 25, which is the beginning of the tune's final eight-measure B phrase. Again, like Coltrane, Shorter takes a more elastic approach in improvising—his phrases do not follow a predictable pattern of length, but seem to compress or expand at will, and he waits until the very end of his solo to resolve the tension that he has created by improvising across the tune's phrase structure.

In the previous analysis of John Coltrane's "Blues by Five" solo, we saw that the '50s rhythm section responded to Coltrane's formal ambiguity by strongly demarcating the tune's structural boundaries. This contrasts with the way that the '60s rhythm section responds to Shorter's solo. Rather than balancing out Shorter's fluctuating phrases by emphasizing the tune's recurring eight-measure phrase structure, the rhythm section instead "goes with the flow" created by Shorter,

Figure 3.23.   "E.S.P.," Wayne Shorter's solo, second chorus.

strongly marking the beginning of each of his phrases, and, along with Shorter, floats over the tune's structural boundaries. The arrows on line *c* of figure 3.24 designate strong structural markers played by the rhythm section, and these markers coincide with the onset of

Figure 3.23. (continued)

each of Shorter's phrases. Both pianist Herbie Hancock and drummer Tony Williams mark the beginning of Shorter's eight-measure phrase in m. 5—Hancock by playing a strong chord voicing, Williams by hitting his crash cymbal. Both rhythm section members similarly

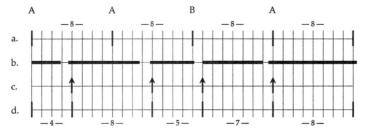

Figure 3.24. Graphic representation of phrase structure, Wayne Shorter, "E.S.P."

mark the beginning of Shorter's five-measure phrase in m. 13. In m. 18, Hancock alone marks the beginning of Shorter's seven-measure phrase, and at this point, both of these musicians set up an interesting polymetric pattern—Shorter plays a melody that implies 3/4 time, while Hancock reinforces this metric superimposition by playing a strong chord voicing every three beats for the next two measures. This example shows that the musicians in this performance coordinate their parts not only to blur the phrase structure of the tune, but also, at times, to blur the basic metric structure as well. Lastly, in m. 25, Hancock and Williams very strongly define the beginning of Shorter's final phrase, and in doing so emphasize the improvisation's return to alignment with the tune's phrase structure, resolving some of the ambiguity in order to set up the next improvised solo.

Conclusion

The two examples considered above—"Blues by Five" and "E.S.P."—demonstrate a range of possibilities for keeping the form. The soloists examined take different approaches; Miles Davis stays close to both the harmonic progression as well as the phrase structure of the tune, while John Coltrane and Wayne Shorter both follow the harmony but improvise over and around the phrase structure. The two rhythm sections also take different approaches to their supporting roles; the '50s Garland–Chambers–Jones rhythm section balances out the soloist in "Blues by Five" by emphasizing the phrase structure when the soloist obscures it, while the '60s Hancock–Carter–Williams rhythm section goes along with the soloist, demarcating the alternate phrase structure created by the soloist's improvisation. For the listener, the two different styles sound very different. The '50s performance sounds very structured and logical; a listener would have no problem keeping track of the form, which is very clearly laid out between the soloist and the rhythm section. In listening to the performance of "E.S.P.," all but the most experienced listeners have a very difficult time keeping track of the form, and because the rhythm section coordinates their structural markers with the soloist's improvised phrases, the listener's perception of the piece's phrase structure will more than likely be something like that shown in line *d* in figure 3.24. That is, the listener would not hear a logical, predictable succession of equal-length phrases, but instead would hear the music as a stream of consciousness. These different approaches invite interesting social and cultural comparisons. For example, in allowing the regular, predictable phrase structure of the tune to exert control over the performance of "Blues by Five," the '50s quintet's performance can be read as a musical analogue to the pressure for social conformity that characterizes the cultural milieu of the 1950s. Likewise, the suppression and subversion of the external, controlling phrase structure in the '60s quintet's performance of "E.S.P."—as well as the on-the-fly establishment of an alternate phrase structure negotiated through group activity—mirrors the social and cultural upheaval taking place at that time.

4

BREAKING DOWN THE BOUNDARIES

Steps toward Free Jazz

All of the performances examined so far have a number of things in common: (1) each features an ensemble consisting of a rhythm section plus one or more additional instruments, (2) the musicians in each performance fulfill certain predefined, standardized roles in their ensembles, (3) each performance follows the common practice of the head arrangement, and (4) each is based on a tune consisting of a melody plus harmonic progression. Taken together, these characteristics represent a sort of "standard practice" for small-group jazz performances; for lack of a better term, I would like to use the term "standard-practice jazz" to describe performances that conform to these criteria. This generic term can be applied to many jazz performances in a number of different styles, including swing, bebop, cool jazz, hard bop, and post bop. While a vast number of small-group jazz performances could be described as standard-practice jazz, many performances also break away from these constraints, and these performances are often described as "free jazz."

Standard-practice jazz and free jazz are often described as being almost diametrically opposed. Historians and critics tend to define free jazz by comparing it with the style or styles that preceded it. In the *Concise Guide to Jazz*, for example, Mark Gridley claims that "free jazz gets its name from the fact that the musicians are improvising jazz that is free from preset chord progressions."[1] James Lincoln Collier expands on this idea, explaining that free-jazz musicians "were all motivated by one idea: to 'free' jazz from what they saw as restrictions of chords, ordinary harmony, bar lines, and even the tempered scale."[2]

Along these same lines, David Such, who prefers the term "out jazz," writes as follows:

> Out jazz tends to lack three major ingredients basic to hard bop (and a number of other styles of jazz), which has been the dominant jazz style since the mid-1950s. These are (1) melodic lines that conform to a chord structure, (2) swing feeling, and (3) adherence to either a twelve-bar or thirty-two-bar form.[3]

A significant problem with these definitions is that they define free jazz negatively; that is, they define it in terms of what it *isn't* rather than what it *is*. Similarly, in *Jazz: A History*, Frank Tirro's description of Ornette Coleman's music also defines free jazz negatively. But rather than limiting himself to a description of free jazz's absence of concrete musical elements, he frames his negative definition in social and cultural terms:

> When a black jazz saxophonist came to New York in 1959 playing an eccentric style of improvised music that rejected traditional norms—music that declared itself free of melodic, harmonic, and metric constraints and that seemed to epitomize an aesthetic of anarchy and nihilism—young musicians of the black community throughout America declared this sound 'our thang.'[4]

While Tirro's social and cultural justification of the negative definition of free jazz is slightly more sophisticated than the others—he argues that by rejecting traditional musical constraints, free jazz is symbolic of a broader social and cultural movement—he still doesn't define what free jazz *is*. If, as these authors would have us believe, the goal of free jazz is simply to reject the musical factors that constrained previous styles of jazz, how is it that we still hear it as jazz? In other words, what about free jazz allows us to hear it as a continuation of standard-practice jazz rather than its negation?

The simple schematic diagram in figure 4.1 allows us to compare free jazz (as defined by these authors) with standard-practice jazz. This diagram maps the characteristic relationship between the performers and various organizing musical materials. The left-to-right arrow marked "Standard-practice Jazz" describes a performance in which the organizing musical materials have a controlling (if not determining)

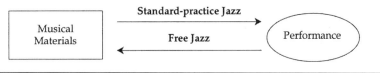

Figure 4.1.   Schematic, Standard-practice Jazz vs. Free Jazz.

effect; the musicians create their individual parts within a range of possibilities defined by formal aspects of the tune being performed, as well as standard performance practices. The right-to-left arrow labeled "Free Jazz," on the other hand, reverses this relationship; rather than exerting a controlling influence over the performers, musical materials are instead determined over the course of the performance through communication and negotiation between the musicians.

What these authors's definitions fail to consider is the interactive nature of jazz performance. As modeled in chapter 1, the improvisational process involves musicians simultaneously deciding what to play, playing it, hearing what the other musicians in the ensemble are playing, and possibly modifying subsequent decisions about what to play based on what they hear. This process is essentially the same in both standard-practice jazz and free jazz. The crucial difference is one of priority or emphasis: in standard-practice jazz, the musicians carry out this interactive improvisational process in relation to a predefined tune and standardized performance practices, and within these constraints, transform the materials being performed. Likewise, in free jazz the musicians also respond to one another, but rather than playing off of and transforming precomposed materials, the musicians engage in a process of continual interaction in which each musician's improvised output takes the place of a precomposed tune. In other words, a free-jazz performance is a self-altering process: the musical materials improvised by each musician re-enter the system, potentially serving as input to which the other performers may respond.

Comparing standard-practice jazz and free jazz in this way allows us to talk about what they have in common, rather than merely describe how they differ. Namely, both styles involve interactive improvisational performances in which the musicians transform musical materials, and the main difference lies in the source of these materials: in standard-practice jazz, the musicians transform predefined materials, and in free jazz the musicians transform materials improvised in the course of the performance. While free jazz can be viewed as a negation of standard-practice jazz, as the authors above seem to imply, it can also be heard as a completion or fulfillment—a Hegelian *Aufhebung*—of the improvisational and creative impulses evident in standard-practice jazz. If we view improvisation as the most important aspect—possibly even the essence—of jazz, then free jazz presents this essence in its purest form by stripping away less essential aspects, such as predefined melodies, chord progressions, phrase structures, and performance practices, replacing them with an intensified focus on the interactive improvisational process.

While this view counters the definition of free jazz as a radical break or disruption from previous traditions, the differences between the styles cannot be ignored; the inversion of the relationship between organizing musical elements and an improvised performance, diagrammed in figure 4.1, still holds, and free jazz does, at the very least, represent a fairly radical reconfiguration of the performance process. Considering this relationship between these styles raises an important question: while free jazz can be seen as the simultaneous negation and completion of certain musical tendencies inherent in standard-practice jazz, how did this process occur? Did free jazz evolve gradually from standard-practice jazz, or was the reconfiguration of the performance process the equivalent of an overnight revolution, a musical coup d'état? In response to these questions, in this final chapter I argue that free jazz evolved from standard-practice jazz through a gradual breaking down of predefined musical parameters, and, furthermore, that it is possible to discern a number of discrete steps in this process of moving away from standard-practice jazz and toward free jazz. We will see that moving away from predefined musical parameters often (but not always) creates a need for heightened interaction between musicians. I will consider three pieces that lie somewhere in between standard-practice jazz and free jazz. Each of these pieces moves toward free jazz by breaking down one particular musical parameter, and the analyses will focus specifically on the ways that the musicians interact and coordinate their improvised parts to negotiate the parameter left undefined. The chapter ends with a brief discussion and comparison of two free-jazz performances.

Bill Evans's "Autumn Leaves"

The Bill Evans Trio's 1959 recording of "Autumn Leaves" moves toward free jazz by breaking down the performance practices of the head arrangement and freeing up the standard instrumental roles in the ensemble.[5] Rather than following the standard "head – piano solo – bass solo – drum solo – head" format, this ensemble takes a more flexible approach. In parts of this performance, the improvisations are not rigidly segmented; the musicians do not always take turns improvising, but rather engage in a free-flowing musical conversation in which all three musicians may improvise simultaneously. This particular trio, composed of Bill Evans, piano, Scott LaFaro, bass, and Paul Motian, drums, is famous for just such a flexible and communicative approach.

Before turning to this improvisation on "Autumn Leaves," I would like to first examine the composition itself, briefly discussing some possible improvisational strategies. Figure 4.2 contains the opening motive and the harmonic progression of "Autumn Leaves." The tune is thirty-two measures long and breaks neatly into two sixteen-measure sections.[6]

The A section, which extends through mm. 1–16, consists of an eight-measure phrase that repeats, with only a slight change at the end of the second phrase to allow the melody to end on G, the tonic pitch class. The B section, which extends through mm. 17–32, then breaks into four four-measure phrases; but because the first three of these phrases do not convey a strong sense of closure, this section sounds much more through-composed. One possible strategy for improvising on this composition might be to base one's improvisation on the tune itself as well as on the more elemental "genetic blueprint" of its underlying voice-leading. Figure 4.3a, which shows this underlying voice-leading, confirms the above description of this tune's form.[7] In the A section (mm. 1–16), the melody essentially repeats itself, descending from E♭ to B♭ in the first phrase, and repeating this motion in the second phrase before continuing, a bit less patiently this time, to G. Because both phrases begin the same way and only differ in the degree of closure they create in their final measures, this first part feels sectionalized; there is a sense of starting over in m. 9,

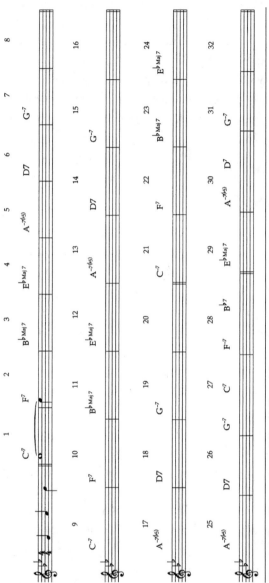

Figure 4.2. "Autumn Leaves" (Joseph Kosma), harmonic progression and opening motive.

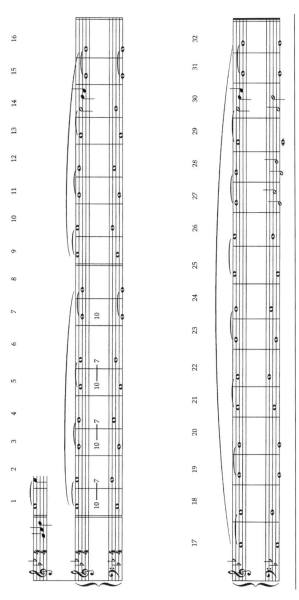

Figure 4.3a.   "Autumn Leaves," underlying voice-leading.

although on the repeat things progress just a little further than in the first phrase.

The B section (mm. 17–32), on the other hand, contrasts with the sectionalized, repetitive feeling of the A section by flowing all the way to the end of the piece. It does this by coordinating its phrases to create a larger melodic gesture that ascends stepwise from G in m. 17 to E♭ in m. 25, before again descending by stepwise motion to a final cadence on G in m. 31. While this section does indeed contrast with the preceding A section, it does so not by bringing in entirely new material, but rather by transforming and recontextualizing the familiar materials of the A section.

Figure 4.3b shows how each phrase is motivically related to the opening of the tune. The tune opens with the *ascending* subdivided minor 6th G–B♭–E♭ (boxed in the example) and the first phrase (mm. 1–8) *descends* stepwise through the second part of this motive, the perfect 4th E♭–B♭, as shown by the beam. The second phrase continues this development of the opening motive, filling in the entire minor 6th by descending from E♭ in m. 9 all the way to G in m. 15. The B section also relates to this motive, ascending by stepwise motion from G in m. 16 to E♭ in m. 25. When the B section melody finally reaches its climax—the E♭ in m. 25—its voice-leading continuation matches that of mm. 9–16, descending by step to G in m. 31. The harmonic progression of the B section also recalls that of the A section: it begins by repeating the last four measures of the A section's harmonic progression in mm. 17–20, and beginning in m. 21, the harmonic progression duplicates that of the A section exactly.

This imitation of the A section's melodic descent as well as its harmonic progression doesn't simply create a repetition of the A section's second phrase, however, because these elements are out of phase with one another. The repetitions of both the melodic descent and the harmonic progression are bracketed in figure 4.3c, and under these brackets are numbers in parentheses that designate the corresponding measures from the A section's second phrase. This example shows that when the melody reaches its apex in m. 25 and the descent from E♭ to G starts over, the harmonic progression is already halfway through; thus, the melody at this point is transformed through reharmonization. Furthermore, this reharmonization causes a significant change

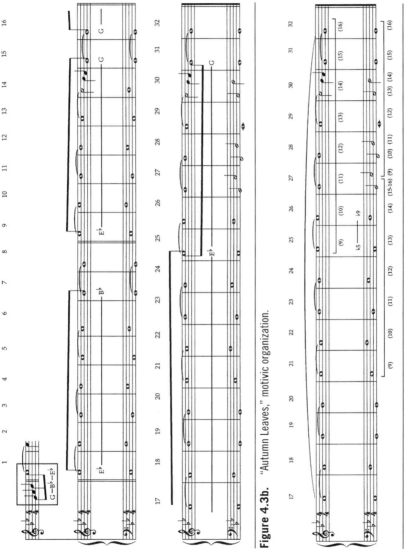

Figure 4.3b. "Autumn Leaves," motivic organization.

Figure 4.3c. Voice-leading, "Autumn Leaves," mm. 17–32.

in the way the melody feels. When the melody descended from E♭ in the A section, it took part in a voice-leading pattern with the bass that alternated consonant 10ths with dissonant 7ths. In the B section, however, the initial E♭ (in m. 25) forms a dissonant diminished 5th with the A in the bass, and when held across the barline forms another dissonance, this time a minor 9th with the bass D. This transformation of E♭ from an initial consonance to a dissonance destabilizes the tune and propels it forward from its melodic apex, a sense of forward motion further enhanced by the intensification of the rate of the harmonic progression beginning in m. 27. Here, the bass line of the A section again repeats and, besides contributing to the sense of flowing forward to the end, the doubling of the harmonic rhythm also allows the melody and harmonic progression to get back into phase with one another, to realign in time to end together.

Another way of improvising over this tune is to improvise on its harmonic progression, and one way of improvising on a harmonic progression is to "run the changes," that is, to focus on each chord as it goes by, creating a melody that conforms to that chord. An improviser may also consider a series of chords and construct a single line that interconnects or weaves through the entire series. When improvising in this manner, jazz musicians will often look for common harmonic patterns to help them understand how the piece is organized. Examining the harmony of the first phrase (mm. 1–8) of "Autumn Leaves" reveals a "circle-of-fifths" progression in the key of G minor. As can be seen in figure 4.4a, the harmony of this phrase cycles, Sechter-like, through all of the diatonic harmonies of G minor: IV–VII–III–VI–II–V–I.[8] While all of these harmonies do indeed come from G minor, the first three harmonies—C^{-7}–F^7–B♭^{Maj7}, or II–V–I in the key of B♭ major—strongly establish the relative major as an important secondary emphasis. Revising the description of the chord progression to show movement through B♭ major and G minor results in the analysis shown in figure 4.4b.

This example interprets the harmonic progression as two different II–V–I progressions—one in B♭ major, the other in G minor—linked by a common E♭^{Maj7}, which could be interpreted as either IV in B♭ major or VI in G minor. This progression is then repeated in the

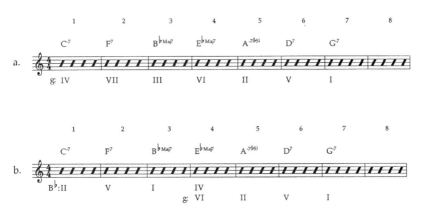

Figure 4.4. Analysis of harmonic progression, "Autumn Leaves," mm. 1–8.

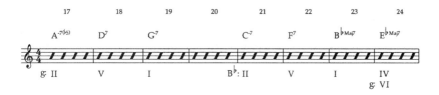

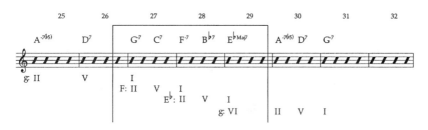

Figure 4.5. Analysis of harmonic progression, "Autumn Leaves," mm. 17–32.

tune's second phrase, mm. 9–16. The B section, analyzed in figure 4.5, reverses the order of the II–V–I progressions; rather than beginning in B♭ major and then moving to G minor, this section begins in G minor and then moves to B♭ major. Nevertheless, with only one two-measure exception, the harmonic progression throughout the B section remains entirely in B♭ major and G minor. The exception occurs in mm. 27–28, which serves to connect G⁻⁷ at the beginning of m. 27 with E♭^Maj7 in m. 29. The analysis in figure 4.5 shows how this connection occurs. While G⁻⁷ on the downbeat of m. 27 is the goal of the preceding II–V progression, the movement to C⁷ allows it to be reinterpreted as II in F major, which is then followed by V. This movement from the diatonic II to V in F major leads us to expect a resolution to I, the tonic F major harmony. This II–V progression does indeed resolve to I, but this resolution is somewhat destabilized in that the chord of resolution is a surprising F^{-7} rather than the expected F^{Maj7}. This harmony is then followed by $B\flat^7$, which allows it to be similarly reinterpreted as a II chord, creating a II–V progression leading to $E\flat^{Maj7}$ in m. 29. At this point, the progression again heads toward the final goal of G minor, which arrives in m. 31.

Thinking of the harmonic progression of "Autumn Leaves" in this way—that is, as a series of diatonic harmonic sequences—allows a jazz musician to develop another improvisational strategy. By thinking of a series of harmonies as belonging to a specific key, the musician can broaden his or her vision beyond each individual chord and think in broader musical swatches. For example, when improvising over the first four measures, the musician can simply focus on $B\flat$ major pitches, rather than on each individual harmony as it goes by. Likewise, in mm. 5–8, which consists of a II–V–I in G minor, the musician can improvise a melody based on the notes of G minor. Furthermore, by realizing that $B\flat$ major and G minor are relatives of one another, and therefore share the same signature, a musician can take an even broader perspective, and simply think of a key signature consisting of $B\flat$ and $E\flat$ through the entire first phrase. And since all but two measures of the piece (mm. 27–28) are based on these two keys, one can think this way through virtually the entire composition.[9]

The two ways of improvising on a tune's harmonic progression described above—focusing on individual chords and focusing on key centers—are of course not mutually exclusive. In fact, a powerful improvisational strategy reconciles these two approaches by considering the voice-leading of the harmonic progression itself—as opposed to that of the melody, considered previously—and using it to guide one's improvised melody through the pitches of each tonal zone. Figure 4.6 sketches the harmonic voice-leading of the first phrase, mm. 1–8. As the progression moves from chord to chord, roots and 3rds sustain across the barline, becoming 5ths and 7ths, while 5ths and 7ths descend by step to become roots and 3rds. By choosing notes from the key that emphasize these melodic connections between

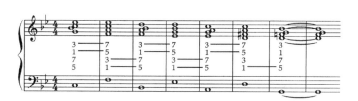

Figure 4.6. Voice-leading of harmonic progression, "Autumn Leaves," mm. 1–8.

chords, an improviser can create strong melodies. In fact, as we heard earlier (figure 4.3a), the first two phrases of the composed melody of "Autumn Leaves" behave exactly this way: they are based on a series of 3rds (or 10ths), each of which are held over to become the 7th of the next chord, which then resolve down by step to the 3rd of the following chord, and so on.

I would like to consider one final improvisational strategy before turning to the transcribed performance of "Autumn Leaves," and that is a strategy of creating coherence through the repetition and development of motives. A number of scholars have written about the ways jazz musicians construct improvised melodies with this strategy: in "Charlie Parker: Techniques of Improvisation," Thomas Owens analyzes a large collection of Parker's improvisations, showing that much of his improvisation can be explained through the stringing together and manipulation of a relatively small number of motives.[10] In "Sonny Rollins and the Challenge of Thematic Improvisation," Gunther Schuller also sees motivic repetition and development as key to Sonny Rollins's improvised solo on "Blue Seven."[11] While both authors emphasize the importance of motivic organization, their arguments are slightly different: Owens describes a set of motives Charlie Parker uses throughout his entire recorded output—certain motives show up over and over again, in different improvisations— while Schuller describes Rollins's improvisational manipulation of motives as a unique characteristic of that particular solo. Figure 4.7 very briefly demonstrates this improvisational strategy; we will see many more examples in the analyses that follow. In this figure, from the beginning of Bill Evans's improvisation on "Autumn Leaves," we can hear that he develops his improvised melody motivically; after his opening descending seventh chord arpeggiation, he continues

Figure 4.7. Bill Evans, "Autumn Leaves," mm. 1.9–1.12.

his improvisation by stringing together transposed and rhythmically transformed motivic echoes of this gesture.

We will see that all of these strategies (as well as others) come into play in this excerpt from the Bill Evans Trio's performance of "Autumn Leaves." Furthermore, since we will be considering all three improvised parts—piano, bass, and drums—we will also see that each musician is frequently influenced by the others, often improvising in a manner that imitates, complements, or in some way responds to the other musicians' simultaneous improvisations. The excerpt, which is transcribed in figure 4.8, follows the initial statement of the head.

As mentioned previously, if this performance were a traditional head arrangement, the head would be followed by an orderly series of solos by each musician in the group. However, this performance breaks from the common practice of the head arrangement by following the head with a section in which all three musicians improvise simultaneously. Also, in this excerpt the musicians don't consistently fulfill their normative roles in the ensemble: bassist LaFaro doesn't walk, pianist Evans doesn't play chords, and drummer Motian doesn't keep time with repetitive rhythmic patterns. On the contrary, LaFaro and Evans improvise melodies in counterpoint with each other, and Motian only occasionally provides a sparse, percussive commentary.

The interaction is most intense between LaFaro and Evans, and their improvisations can be heard as an energetic musical conversation; there is a continual give-and-take between them, and their phrases usually dovetail, creating a sense of continual motion and interplay. In analyzing this transcription, I would like to take an in-time approach, considering several dovetailed pairs of phrases in turn, describing the improvisational strategies that seem to influence each musician, as well as exploring any relationships between their individual improvised lines. Because the phrases do usually overlap, examining each pair of phrases will involve considering each individual phrase twice:

Figure 4.8. Bill Evans Trio's group improvisation on "Autumn Leaves."

once as a phrase that responds to the preceding phrase, and once as an initiating phrase that is responded to by the subsequent phrase. That is, if the bass and piano phrases continually overlap, we will first consider the relationship, say, between the bassist's first phrase and the pianist's first phrase, then the relationship between the pianist's first phrase and the bassist's *second* phrase, and so on, leapfrogging through the excerpt.

Figure 4.9 transcribes the beginning of this section. The measures in the following examples are numbered to show where the musicians are in the thirty-two-measure form of the tune; after the initial two-measure break, the entire excerpt is two choruses long, so descriptions

Figure 4.8. (continued)

of the location of an example in the excerpt will designate both the chorus number (1 or 2) and the measure number (1–32): m. 1.9, then, will designate the ninth measure of the first chorus, m. 2.3 the third measure of the second chorus, and so on.

Bassist LaFaro begins this section by taking a two-measure break that he uses to set up his solo over the first eight-measure phrase of the form, mm. 1.1–8. He uses a variety of improvisational strategies and introduces a number of motives in this section. He begins by emphasizing the note D, which, as both the 5th of the underlying harmony, G^{-7}, and the 5th scale degree in G minor, is harmonically significant

Figure 4.8. (continued)

both locally and globally. He follows this with a "bluesy" motive that revolves around C. This motive, bracketed in figure 4.9, sounds bluesy because it is made up of pitches from the G blues scale: B♭ is the minor 3rd, C the fourth, and D♭ the diminished 5th.[12] Since this motive revolves around C, it smoothly leads into the C^{-7} that begins the first chorus. In m. 1.1, LaFaro bases his improvisation on the harmony of the moment by arpeggiating down this C^{-7} harmony. Moving into m. 1.2, he seems to think more globally, improvising a melody that fills in the preceding descending arpeggiation by running up a scale based primarily on the overall key center. His improvised melody at

Figure 4.8. (continued)

this point doesn't strongly convey F⁷; in fact, since it emphasizes the pitches E♭ and C, it seems to extend the C⁻⁷ of the previous measure. In mm. 1.3–4, LaFaro's melody becomes more motivically based: the descending C–A 3rd on the first beat is followed by a filled-in 3rd that ascends from D to F, which is followed by the descending 3rd F–D, which is in turn followed by a filled-in 3rd that descends from E♭ to C. In mm. 1.5 and 1.6, the descending arpeggiation of an F♯°⁷ chord again shows evidence of a more global approach to harmony: rather than improvising a line that clearly defines the A⁻⁷⁽♭⁵⁾ and D⁷ harmonies, LaFaro treats both measures as leading to the G-minor

Figure 4.8. (continued)

goal, which, interestingly, he does not acknowledge in m. 1.7. Rather, he elides this G^{-7}, sustaining the C and linking the preceding harmony with the following reiteration of the opening bluesy motive, which is again used as it was before, to set up the move to C^{-7} that begins the next phrase. The fact that LaFaro doesn't explicitly define the individual harmonies throughout this example doesn't mean that these harmonies are not in effect; since this improvised section follows a performance of the entire tune complete with its harmonic progression, the listener has heard this progression and can keep it in mind while listening to LaFaro's improvisation.

Figure 4.8. (continued)

Figure 4.9. "Autumn Leaves," break and mm. 1.1–1.8.

Throughout this opening section, LaFaro uses an interesting and balanced variety of improvisational strategies: at times, he relates the content of his improvisation to the local harmony, at other times he thinks more globally; at times, he spins out a melody based on the key center, at other times he develops his line more motivically. Furthermore, in his improvisation he seems to seek a continual balance between contrast and repetition in the way that he chooses to continue and respond to a given musical gesture. For example, he complements his descending arpeggiation in m. 1.1 with a stepwise melody that ascends through the same register, even emphasizing many of the same pitches, in m. 1.2. In other words, this ascending gesture can be heard as a complementary transformation (and thus a coherent continuation) of the previous gesture. Likewise, the ascending line in m. 1.2 leads to the downbeat of m. 1.3 with a leap of a 3rd from A to C, and LaFaro continues his improvisation in mm. 1.3–4 by developing this interval motivically. In mm. 1.5–6, he continues to base his improvisation on this motive, this time stringing 3rds together to create a descending arpeggiated seventh chord, which also recalls the earlier descending arpeggiation in m. 1.1. Finally, he strips away the lower pitches of this descending seventh chord, boiling it down to the single pitch C, which he uses to move into a bluesy gesture that recalls the way he began this section. We will see that both LaFaro and Evans combine all of these ways of improvising throughout the remainder of the excerpt, and that not only do they develop their individual improvised melodies as LaFaro did in this opening section—that is, by continually imitating, transforming, and complementing previous gestures—but they also develop and transform each other's motives and gestures. In other words—true to the improvisational process outlined in chapter 1— these musicians structure and organize their improvised performance by continually responding to the gestures and motives of both their own improvised solos as well as those of the others in the ensemble, and because in this performance these responses are freed from the constraints of standardized instrumental roles, the musicians are free to respond to one another melodically, using processes of motivic and gestural imitation, transformation, and contrast.

Figure 4.10. "Autumn Leaves," mm. 1.9–1.12.

In figure 4.10, Evans joins LaFaro in musical conversation. This excerpt comes from the beginning of the second phrase of the A section (mm. 1.9–12), which cycles through the same harmonic progression as the previous phrase. LaFaro begins this phrase exactly as he began the previous phrase, by strongly defining C⁻⁷ through a descending arpeggiation. Evans imitates LaFaro's opening gesture, descending through an arpeggiation of the 9th, 7th, 5th, and 3rd of C⁻⁷. Interestingly, while LaFaro and Evans begin on different pitches—Evans on D, LaFaro on C—they both end up on the same pitch class (E♭) on the same beat (beat 3). LaFaro then plays an ascending scalar line, which Evans complements with a descending series of arpeggiations. With these complementary gestures—LaFaro's ascent and Evans's descent—the music contracts inward, contributing to the sense of closure created by Evans's motion toward and arrival on the tonic G in m. 1.12.

Besides this gestural complementation, two factors seem to control Evans's improvisation in this phrase: (1) motivic development of his opening gesture, which itself was also in response to LaFaro's improvisation, and (2) the prominent pitches of the tune's melody and its underlying voice-leading, as illustrated in figure 4.11. The goal of both Evans's and LaFaro's opening arpeggiation is E♭, which is the note that the tune sustains at this point. In the voice-leading sketch of figure 4.3b, we heard the A section's emphasis on the melodic descent from E♭ to B♭. As shown by the beaming in mm. 1.10–12 of figure 4.11, Evans brings out a smaller-scale replication of this voice-leading pattern, one that takes place within the space of two measures, rather than over the course of the entire eight-measure phrase. Evans repeats the descending arpeggiated motive beginning on the upper

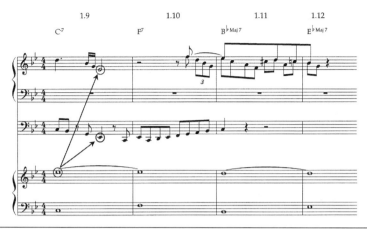

Figure 4.11. "Autumn Leaves," mm. 1.9–1.12.

neighbor F, which leads to the significant (in terms of voice-leading) pitch E♭. He then embellishes the descending D–C–B♭ continuation with a lower neighbor and chord leaps. Evans uses this embellished D–C–B♭ descent motivically throughout the rest of his improvisation, frequently to signal the ends of phrases. In a sense, Evans's transformation of the underlying voice-leading descent E♭–D–C–B♭ into motivic material itself can be read as an analysis of the tune; Evans pulls this essential background figure into the foreground, using it to structure his improvisation.

In figure 4.12, we can see LaFaro's response to Evans's improvised phrase. LaFaro responds to Evans's descending D–C–B♭ motive by *ascending* through the same pitches in m. 1.12, even incorporating Evans's C♯ chromatic lower neighbor to D. The rest of LaFaro's phrase also seems influenced by Evans's closing gesture. On beat 3 of m. 1.12, LaFaro descends through D–C–B♭; he then plays a line

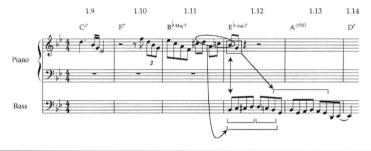

Figure 4.12. "Autumn Leaves," mm. 1.9–1.14.

Figure 4.13. "Autumn Leaves," mm. 1.12–1.16.

that revolves around the pitches Bb and G, the final pitches of Evans's phrase. The transition between Evans's and LaFaro's phrases in this excerpt is almost seamless: LaFaro not only develops ideas that Evans had introduced just moments before, but also enters on the exact same pitch—Bb—that Evans is playing. The resulting musical effect is that of a single improvised melody split between two different instruments.

Figure 4.13 leapfrogs to the next pair of phrases: LaFaro's phrase, discussed in figure 4.12, and Evans's subsequent response. Here, we see another example of seamless integration: as shown by the arrows in the figure, Evans begins his phrase by playing the same pitches as LaFaro: D and Eb. This may have been more than mere chance. LaFaro, improvising a line descending to D, could have heard that Evans was beginning an ascending line, and when both players reached D on beat 4, LaFaro could have quickly changed direction to imitate the gesture begun by Evans. As in the previous phrase, Evans picks up a motive previously introduced by LaFaro, specifically, the "bluesy" motive centering on the pitches Db, C, and Bb, bracketed in the example. The peak of Evans's long, arching line centers on these pitches, and he transforms this climactic melodic figure into cadential arpeggiation in the next measure, where it occurs in a lower register, acknowledging the arrival on G. Furthermore, in improvising a line that begins by ascending, Evans again complements the overall descent of LaFaro's gesture, this time creating a feeling of registral expansion; the music seems to open up and pull apart, creating a tension that propels Evans's melody forward to its "bluesy" peak before it comes crashing down, returning to the lower register.

Figure 4.14 moves to the next pair of phrases. Here, LaFaro gets swept along with Evans's rapid descent, imitating his long descending gesture; in fact, the coordination of these fast descending lines creates such a strong sense of momentum that LaFaro's melody is propelled forward even though Evans comes to a close on G in m. 1.16. LaFaro's momentum is so strong that he overshoots the G tonic in m. 1.16, and works his way back up to this pitch by repeating the same ascending scalar motive (boxed in the figure) he had played previously in m. 1.2 and again in m. 1.10. Interestingly, when LaFaro previously played this motive, it was over F^7; here, the harmony is $A^{-7(b5)}$. This is another example of how LaFaro tends to balance chord-to-chord thinking with the improvisational strategies of motivic repetition and development as well as playing on the key-center throughout his improvisation. Once he arrives on G in m. 1.18, LaFaro doesn't stop abruptly, but plays a zigzagging line that allows the momentum to dissipate more gradually. His melody at this point fills in the minor 3rd G–B♭, recalling the motivic idea he introduced in m. 1.13 of the previous phrase, which was itself in response to the closing gesture of Evans's first phrase.

In figure 4.15, Evans responds by imitating LaFaro's gesture from m. 1.17, as annotated in the figure with the boxes and arrow. While Evans's gesture in m. 1.18 doesn't *exactly* match LaFaro's, it seems to retain some essential aspects of its character: LaFaro's gesture begins by winding around within a small range before ascending, as does Evans's. Both LaFaro's and Evans's gestures begin their ascent by an ascending chromatic motion: C–C♯ in the case of LaFaro, F–F♯ in the case of Evans. Both gestures subsequently ascend, LaFaro's by stepwise motion, Evans's by inverting an earlier motive—a descending seventh chord—and arpeggiating an F♯ diminished seventh. Evans rounds out his phrase by again recalling the descending D–C–B♭ closing motive he previously introduced. At this point, Paul Motian enters, responding to the composite motoric string of eighth notes created between Evans and LaFaro.

Continuing into figure 4.16, we hear a number of interesting interactions. LaFaro begins his phrase in m. 1.19 by again picking up (and inverting) Evans's closing B♭–G motive. He then ascends to F, which he repeats across the barline from m. 1.20 to m. 1.21, before ascending to B♭, the local goal. Evans responds to both LaFaro and Motian when he enters in m. 21. He picks up on LaFaro's repeated F

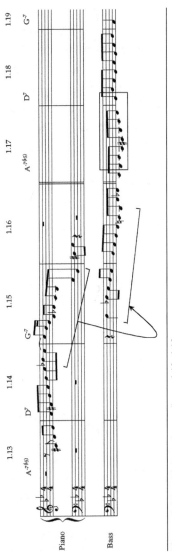

Figure 4.14. "Autumn Leaves," mm. 1.13–1.19.

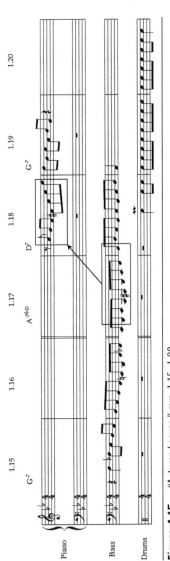

Figure 4.15. "Autumn Leaves," mm. 1.15–1.20.

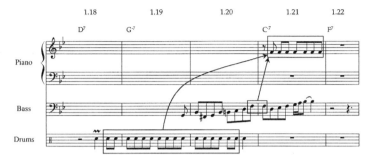

Figure 4.16.   "Autumn Leaves," mm. 1.18–1.22.

and continues by repeating that same pitch. By repeating the same pitch, he also seems to be responding to Motian's string of eighth notes, de-emphasizing melodic contour and focusing on rhythm alone. At this point, we have the first significant break in the texture since this improvised section began. It's almost as if LaFaro and Evans were so focused on responding to each other and to Motian that neither one was thinking about how the music would progress from this point, or who would take the lead, resulting in the musical equivalent of a traffic jam; everything grinds to a halt.

After almost a full measure of silence, LaFaro jumps in, again taking the lead. As can be seen in figure 4.17, Evans enters by imitating LaFaro's opening gesture before diverging and complementing LaFaro's descending gesture with his own ascending line. Most of the rest of this improvisation continues in this same vein—each musician continues to develop motives introduced by themselves or the others, and imitates or complements each other's melodic gestures; the underlying harmony, tonic, or voice-leading continues to exert varying degrees of influence on the proceedings. Rather than continuing with such a close

Figure 4.17.   "Autumn Leaves," mm. 1.22–1.26.

examination of each set of phrases, which would only reveal more of the same kinds of improvisational strategies and interactions, I would like to focus on just one more selected excerpt in which the conversational interaction between the players is especially heightened.

This excerpt is notated in figure 4.18 and begins one measure before the beginning of the second chorus, that is, in m. 1.32. LaFaro again initiates, playing a motive that begins by embellishing G with chromatic lower neighbors before ascending to B♭. On reaching the B♭, LaFaro sounds as if he's stuck; he keeps zigzagging around within a very narrow range. When Evans enters in m. 2.1, he almost exactly imitates LaFaro's opening motive, with the only difference being the omission of the initial F♯ chromatic lower neighbor. After the first note, Evans and LaFaro coordinate their parts, playing the same notes (F♯–G–A–B♭) through the downbeat of m. 2.2. Evans's entrance and the subsequent coordination of their parts seems to break LaFaro out of his rut; through the end of the phrase, his line takes on more direction and motion and becomes less repetitive. At the B♭ on the downbeat of m. 2, Evans and LaFaro diverge, with Evans changing direction and descending, while LaFaro continues his ascent. On beat 3, they again arrive at the same pitch, F, at which point LaFaro changes direction and again matches exactly what Evans is playing. It's likely that LaFaro's change of direction and subsequent chromatic descent is in response to Evans; LaFaro hears Evans begin a chromatic descent on beat 2, and when the piano and bass lines converge on F on beat 3, he changes direction, assuming that Evans will continue his chromatic descent. Evans does continue, and, as a result, the piano and bass again lock up, playing the same pitches (F–F♭–E♭).

The E♭ goal of both LaFaro's and Evans's descending chromatic line again demonstrates the influence of the underlying voice-leading, as shown in figure 4.19. As before, the E♭ is the significant pitch of the melody at this point, and upon reaching this pitch, Evans stops his descent while LaFaro delays his continuation to D by inserting a chromatic lower neighbor. LaFaro then moves to D on the downbeat of m. 2.3, further emphasizing the underlying voice-leading: the 7th of F^7 (E♭) descends by semitone to the 3rd (D) of the following B♭^{Maj7}. LaFaro's continuation in m. 2.3 again shows evidence that he's

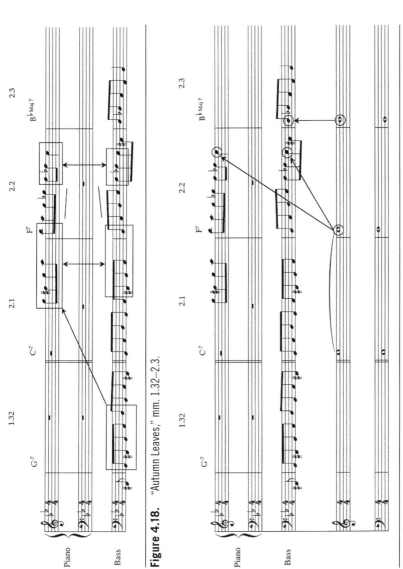

Figure 4.18. "Autumn Leaves," mm. 1.32–2.3.

Figure 4.19. "Autumn Leaves," mm. 1.32–2.3.

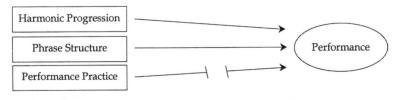

Figure 4.20. Schematic, "Autumn Leaves."

thinking motivically, as he sequences the gesture beginning on beat 2 of m. 2.2 before arriving at the goal of B♭.

Reworking the standard-practice schematic diagram to reflect this performance would result in the example shown in figure 4.20. Here, the organizing musical materials have been split into three distinct parameters: the harmonic progression, the phrase structure, and the performance practices of the head arrangement and standard instrumental roles. In this performance, the harmonic progression and phrase structure still exert a controlling, though at times weakened, force over the performance, but the performance practice of the "head arrangement" and standard instrumental roles have broken down; the musicians may move to the foreground or recede to the background depending on the musical circumstances, and are not always required to fulfill their traditional normative roles in the ensemble. The musicians respond to this breaking down of performance practice by increasing their level of melodic interaction; they engage in an ongoing, free-flowing musical conversation in which ideas are tossed back and forth almost continuously.

Miles Davis's "Flamenco Sketches"

Miles Davis's "Flamenco Sketches," from *Kind of Blue* (1959), takes another step toward free jazz by treating *form* in an innovative way.[13] Bill Evans, the pianist on the recording, described the piece in the album's liner notes as "a series of five scales, each to be played as long as the soloist wishes until he has completed the series." Two things stand out in this description: (1) his description of the composition as a series of "scales," rather than the usual melody plus harmonic progression, and (2) the fact that the length of time spent on each section of the composition is not predetermined, but negotiated between the players in the course of the performance. I would like to briefly discuss the first issue—that of the composition being based on scales—before turning to a more detailed exploration of the second.

The term "modal jazz" is often used to describe jazz performances based on a single scale or a series of scales, and the performances on the album *Kind of Blue* are considered to be some of the first—and certainly some of the most influential—examples of this style. Besides his comments about "Flamenco Sketches," Bill Evans also describes some of the other performances on the album, saying that "So What" is "a simple figure based on 16 measures of one scale, 8 of another, and 8 more of the first," and that "All Blues" is "a 6/8 12-measure blues form that produces its mood through only a few modal changes and Miles Davis's free melodic conception." In a 1958 interview with Nat Hentoff, Davis offered his own view on this subject: "I think a movement in jazz is beginning away from the conventional string of chords, and a return to emphasis on melodic rather than harmonic variation. There will be fewer chords but infinite possibilities as to what to do with them."[14] While Davis does seem to be talking about modal jazz, he describes compositions that are based on a few *chords*, rather than *scales*. In the same interview, he clarifies this, saying that "chords, after all, are relative to scales and certain chords make certain scales." This comment bears a similarity to the ideas expressed in George Russell's well-known *The Lydian Chromatic Concept of Tonal Organization;*[15] in chapter 2, we saw that Russell theorizes a similar relationship between scales and chords. To briefly recap the basic tenet of his theory, Russell claims that scales and chords are intrinsically related, that every chord can be generated from a parent scale, and every scale conveys the quality of a specific harmony. In other words, a chord is simply a vertical realization of a scale, and conversely, a scale is simply a horizontal realization of a chord. Figure 4.21 shows how this works: a D dorian scale and a D^{-7} harmony (with an added 9th, 11th, and 13th) contain the same pitches and are simply two different

Figure 4.21.   Scale/Mode equivalence.

manifestations of the same thing. Of course, defining the dorian scale and the "dorian" chord as equivalent negates the syntactical power of the scale; in effect there's only one chord in the key, and it contains all of the pitches of the scale. As a result, harmonic change is no longer a constructive force, and this music sounds harmonically static.

Various authors writing about modal jazz tend to fall into two different camps. One group accepts this concept of modal jazz at face value and either analyzes performances looking for modal principles or uses the concept to develop pedagogical methods for learning improvisation. Another group views the concept of modal jazz critically, examining performances to see if the label "modal" accurately describes what happens in the music. Barry Kernfeld falls into this second group. In "Adderley, Coltrane and Davis at the Twilight of Bebop: The Search for Melodic Coherence,"[16] Kernfeld says that using the term "modal jazz" to describe the performances on *Kind of Blue* doesn't really work, since the musicians don't restrict themselves solely to the pitches of each mode. In "On Miles and the Modes," William Thomson misinterprets the way jazz musicians use the term "modal," conflating it, strangely, with the ways it was used in medieval and renaissance music. He goes so far as to suggest that the jazz musicians didn't know what they were doing, saying that "Miles Davis and Bill Evans were fooled in their playing of 'So What' into thinking that they were creating a piece in the Dorian mode," and even criticizes Bill Evans for not using the appropriate principles of *musica ficta* in his piano voicings. Thomson declares that while the musicians may have used the pitches of the dorian mode in their performance, "a pitch collection *per se* does not a mode maketh."[17]

The problem with these critiques is that both authors begin with a preconceived notion of what "modal" jazz should be and when the music doesn't behave accordingly they dismiss the concept of modal jazz entirely. In fact, although they approach the subject from different directions, both authors come to similar conclusions, saying these performances aren't substantially different from jazz performances that are considered to be conventionally "tonal"—they hear the succession of long, sustained harmonies as still creating a sense of forward, goal-oriented motion—and therefore to describe modal jazz as a new, qualitatively different style is inaccurate and unwarranted. I think a better approach to defining the term "modal jazz" is to keep in mind Evans's comments regarding the music's being *based* on scales, and study the performances to see how the musicians actually go about basing their performances on each scale. If we do this, we see that "basing" one's improvisation on a scale doesn't necessarily restrict one to pitches of only that scale, that jazz musicians (obviously) use the term "modal" in a different way than did medieval and renaissance musicians, that in fact, for jazz musicians, a pitch collection *does* a mode maketh, and the goal of a modal jazz performance is to explore the characteristic harmonic and melodic qualities inherent in certain specific collections of pitches.

In terms of musical effect and aesthetics, whether we describe the composition as consisting of a series of five scales, modes, or chords is somewhat beside the point. Most important—and this is where I disagree with Kernfeld and Thomson—this music sounds and feels different from music based on more conventional, goal-oriented harmonic progressions. Rather than improvising melodies that weave through a progression, leading to a goal, the musicians are free to inhabit the soundfield created by each scale/mode/harmony for as long as they want, and each mode creates a qualitatively different soundfield for them to explore. The result is a feeling of a succession of static yet colorful blocks of music, and this stasis is a result of treating modes as collections of pitches in a way that relaxes the forward-moving tensions associated with goal-oriented tonal music. Indeed, as we will see in figure 4.22, the "forces of attraction" that medieval and renaissance modes were designed to create, and that, for Fétis, constituted the "immutable laws" of tonality, are no longer in effect; that is, the notion of pitch *centricity* no longer holds a privileged position because the tonic is no longer the *center* of anything. In its place is a more nebulous notion that, for lack of a better term, might be called *bottomness*, in which register takes on the syntactic function that the scale used to have. That is, pitches don't gravitate *toward* the tonic, but rather sound *above* it, and the primacy of the tonic is established through registral means, by being the lowest sounding pitch in the musical texture. Figure 4.22, the C major piano and bass introduction to "Flamenco Sketches," shows how this works. Here, the sense of C as tonic is not created through its semitonal relationship with the leading

Figure 4.22. "Flamenco Sketches," introduction.

tone B, but rather is established through registral emphasis in the bass. This emphasis on C in the bass lays the foundation over which Evans combines the pitches of the C major scale, using various combinations of pitches for their coloristic and expressive qualities rather than for their tendencies to lead to a specific goal. In other words, throughout this section Evans uses the pitch B, for example, not for its tendency to gravitate toward C—it often doesn't—but for the unique color and character it creates when played over the bass C.

After this introduction, the aim of the pianist and bassist throughout this performance is to provide a harmonic environment for the soloist to explore. Furthermore, since the phrase structure of this particular composition is not predetermined, the musicians must all listen to one another and negotiate the change from one section to the next through interaction. In his interview with Nat Hentoff, Miles Davis notes that "when you go this way, you can go on forever. You don't have to worry about [chord] changes and you can do more with the line. It becomes a challenge to see how melodically inventive you are."[18]

Returning to Evans's description of "Flamenco Sketches," what exactly are the five scales in question? In *Free Jazz*, Ekkehard Jost identifies them as (1) C ionian, (2) A♭ ionian, (3) B♭ ionian, (4) D phrygian, (5) G aeolian.[19] As we will see in the transcriptions below, the first section does seem to be based on the pitches of the C ionian (or major) scale and the third section likewise seems to be based on the B♭ ionian (or major) scale. In the second section, however, Bill Evans consistently uses G♭ in his piano voicings, making A♭ mixolydian a better description of the underlying scale. Similarly, both Davis and Evans emphasize E♮ in the final section, making a designation of G dorian more accurate. Deciding on a scale for the

	C Major	A♭ Mixolydian	B♭ Major	D Phrygian (?)	G Dorian
Introduction	4	—	—	—	—
1st Solo: Davis	4	4	4	8	4
2nd Solo: Coltrane	4	4	4	8	5
3rd Solo: Adderley	8	4	8	8	4
4th Solo: Evans	8	4	8	4	4
5th Solo: Davis	4	4	4	8	3

Figure 4.23. Performance map of "Flamenco Sketches."

fourth section is somewhat problematic, since Davis and Evans seem to be basing their parts on at least two different pitch collections. The question of which scale the fourth section is based on will be discussed in the analysis below.

Figure 4.23 maps out the entire performance of "Flamenco Sketches." Interestingly, with only a few exceptions, each soloist remains within each mode for either four or eight measures. This is most likely a result of years spent playing the jazz repertoire in which tunes are almost always composed of four- or eight-measure phrases, resulting in an ingrained sense of "feeling" music in phrases of these lengths. I would like to examine Miles Davis's and John Coltrane's solos, considering both the ways that the musicians play and interact within each mode, and the ways that the musicians negotiate the change from one mode to the next.

Returning to the example in figure 4.22, which transcribes the four-measure introduction to Davis's solo, we see that from the start, Bill Evans and bassist Paul Chambers assume the roles they'll be playing in the performance: Chambers plays simple bass figures that lead to the root of each harmony/mode on the downbeat of each measure, while Evans combines pitches from each mode to create harmonic structures that help to convey its unique "color" or character. Though Evans seems to create his voicings by freely choosing pitches from the C major scale, he tends to emphasize the third scale degree (E) in the first half of the measure and the fourth (F) in the second half, creating a feeling of oscillation, which gives some sense of motion to the relatively static harmonic environment. Furthermore, he also voices his harmonies in a way that creates a gradual registral ascent from m. 1

to m. 4: he begins on E, ascends to F, returns to E, ascends to G, returns to E before ascending through G to B, and finally returns to E and ascends through G and B to the high point of the phrase, D, before descending back down to G. While the pitches in his right hand gradually ascend through mm. 3 and 4, his left hand mirrors this motion, descending into a lower register, creating a broader feeling of expansion and contraction, and—even though the harmonic environment is static—a feeling of gestural and registral tension and relaxation. When Evans reaches the point of greatest expansion, D in m. 4, Miles Davis enters and begins his solo over the first scale, C major, as transcribed in figure 4.24.

Davis begins, moreover, by imitating Evans. As we heard in the introduction, Evans's voicings peaked on D before descending to G. Davis responds by entering on D and, like Evans, resolves the tension created by the registral expansion by also descending to G. Throughout this entire section, Davis develops this opening gesture, continuing the feeling of registral expansion and contraction Evans created in the introduction: at the end of m. 1, Davis improvises an arching line that ascends by step to D before returning to G; in m. 2, he embellishes the D with an upper neighbor before again descending; and finally, in m. 4, he varies the gesture, ending on A instead of G, a musical event Evans and Chambers read as a signal to move on to the next scale.

In figure 4.25, a transcription of the following A♭ mixolydian section, we again hear a strong link between Evans's piano voicings and Davis's improvised melody. Evans's voicing on the downbeat of m. 5 emphasizes the fourth note of the scale (D♭) rather than the third (C), creating a sound often referred to as a "sus," or suspension figure harmony. This name is appropriate for two reasons: (1) this kind of chord is often described as being derived from a 4-3 suspension, although the traditional rules regarding preparation and resolution of the suspension are of course no longer operative in this musical environment; and (2) voicing a harmony in this way creates a static, suspended (in the literal sense of the word) feeling. In this scale especially, by emphasizing the fourth scale degree rather than the third, Evans avoids the strongly forward moving feel of a dominant seventh A♭–C–E♭–G♭, replacing it with a more static sounding "quartal"

Figure 4.24. "Flamenco Sketches," Miles Davis's solo, mm. 1–5.

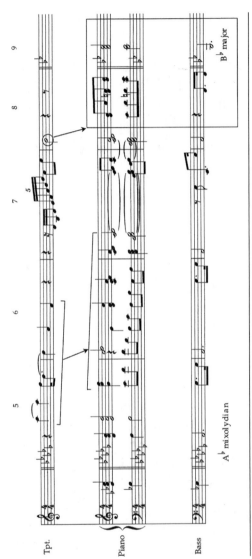

Figure 4.25. "Flamenco Sketches," Miles Davis's solo, mm. 5–9.

A♭–D♭–G♭, which he plays—along with an "additional" B♭—on the downbeat of m. 5.

Davis then reacts to this emphasis on D♭ in Evans's voicings, beginning his phrase with a descent through a D♭ major triad, which in turn encourages Evans to continue to emphasize D♭ in his voicings through the rest of this section. By beginning his phrase in a high register—almost an octave higher than where he ended in the previous section—Davis, playing near the upper boundary of his range, introduces registral and timbral tension that implies a forward-moving descending line, which is exactly what he plays in mm. 5–6. Evans reacts not only to Miles's emphasis on D♭ but also to the shape and quality of his phrase, imitating Davis's descending gesture with the top note of his voicings: on beat 4 of m. 5, Davis and Evans both arrive at F, before Davis completes his downward arpeggiation through the D♭ triad. At this point, Evans changes direction, following Davis down to D♭ on the downbeat of m. 6, and continues to imitate Davis's gesture by playing voicings in which the top notes descend through D♭$^{\text{Maj7}}$. Furthermore, Evans incorporates Davis's implied sense of forward motion into his accompaniment in two ways: first, he improvises a much longer gesture than anything he had previously played, leading from F in m. 5 down to D♭ in m. 7; second, he further enhances the flow by supporting the right hand's descending gesture with a faster eighth-note line in the left hand which also descends through an octave during this same time span.

When Evans reaches the D♭ resting point at the end of his long descending gesture in m. 7, Davis continues his improvisation by responding to his and Evans's descent as well as to Evans's increase in rhythmic motion: he balances the initial descending gestures by improvising an ascending line and he increases his rhythmic activity, accelerating before broadening into the end of the phrase. As in the previous section, Davis ends this section by arriving on a pitch not previously emphasized (B♭ on the downbeat of m. 8), an event Evans and Chambers again interpret as a signal to change to the next scale.

The third section, transcribed in figure 4.26, is based on a B♭ major scale. Here, we see an interesting interaction on the fourth beat of m. 10: both Davis and Chambers play the same rhythm leading to the

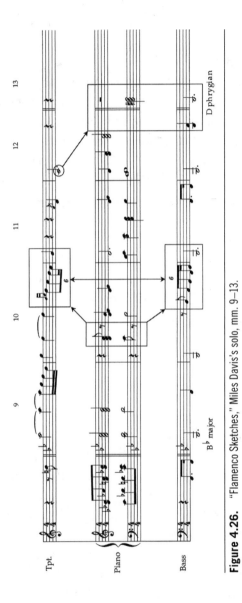

Figure 4.26. "Flamenco Sketches," Miles Davis's solo, mm. 9–13.

downbeat of m. 11, boxed in figure 4.26. Furthermore, this rhythm is not one that has been previously used in this performance, leading one to wonder how these musicians decided to play the same rhythm at the same time. While this could be merely a chance occurrence, a possible answer may lie in Evans's comping earlier in the measure. Up to this point, his comping has been very gentle and soft, with long sustained harmonies played without sharp attacks, often creating a static, suspended feeling. However, on beat 2 of m. 10, he plays a short, *staccato*, slightly accented chord, creating a feeling of rhythmic energy and motion leading to the voicing on beat 3. Davis and Chambers may have been influenced by this increase in rhythmic energy and responded by playing a figure that moves with more energy and motion to the downbeat of m. 11. So, while both may have been reacting to the rhythmic energy and sense of forward motion of Evans's comping, they both happened to react in the same way, playing the same rhythm to lead to the downbeat of m. 11. As in the previous sections, Davis again signals the change to the following section by playing a note that he had not previously emphasized, the long, drawn out C in m. 12.

As discussed earlier, Jost described the scale used in the fourth section as D phrygian, and, as can be seen in figure 4.27, Davis's improvised melody does indeed conform to this collection of pitches. Evans's voicings, on the other hand, tend to oscillate between D major and E♭ major triads, creating the "Flamenco" feel alluded to in the piece's title. The colorful clash between Davis's F♮s and Evans's F♯s creates an interesting tension that sets this section apart; it sounds significantly different from the other sections. In m. 18, Evans stops oscillating between D and E♭, and begins emphasizing the E♭ sonority only, with particular emphasis on the 5th, B♭. Davis responds by moving emphatically to B♭ in m. 20. Once again, by emphasizing a note that he hasn't previously emphasized, Davis signals the end of the section, and Evans and Chambers pick up on Davis's signal, moving smoothly to the next section on the downbeat of the following measure.

In the final section, transcribed in figure 4.28, the top notes of Evans's voicings are again influenced by Davis's improvisation: Davis begins his phrase by emphasizing E (the pitch that confirms that this section is based on G dorian rather than G minor or aeolian, which would include an E♭), and Evans strongly emphasizes this pitch in

Figure 4.27. "Flamenco Sketches," Miles Davis's solo, mm. 13–21.

Figure 4.28. "Flamenco Sketches," Miles Davis's solo, mm. 21–24.

m. 23. Evans also imitates Davis's descent in m. 21 from E to C by voicing his chords in m. 22 so that the pitches E and C are on top. In the final measure of this section, Evans imitates Davis's opening gesture more completely: in m. 21, Davis descends E–C–A–G, and Evans ends this section with the same descent, leading to G on the downbeat of the next measure, which sets up the next solo, that of John Coltrane.

Throughout Davis's solo, two consistent interactive processes take place. First, Davis tends to signal the end of one section (and thus the beginning of the next) by moving to a pitch he hasn't emphasized previously in the section. Second, there are continual two-way interactions between Davis's choice of notes and Evans's piano voicings: sometimes Davis bases his melody on notes of Evans's voicings; sometimes Evans bases his voicings on the prominent notes of Davis's melody. Then again these interactions sometimes dovetail, as we heard in the A♭ mixolydian section, where Davis began by reacting to Evans's emphasis on D♭, and Evans continued by imitating Davis's descending D♭ arpeggiation.

The communication between the players in Davis's solo is on a very high level, resulting in seamless changes from one section to the next. The musicians don't fare as well in John Coltrane's solo, however, and frequently misinterpret each other's cues. I would like to briefly examine Coltrane's solo, transcribed along with Chambers's bass part in figure 4.29, focusing specifically on the changes from one section to the next. Things begin well: Chambers lays down a consistent G–C/dominant–tonic bass line for the first section, strongly defining a C major tonic, and Coltrane improvises a melody that centers on the colorful pitches B (the major 7th) and D (the major 9th).

Close examination of the change from the first section to the next reveals an interesting series of implications, reactions, miscommunications, and error corrections. In fact, it seems as if Coltrane and Chambers, misinterpreting each other's signals, fake each other out. Figure 4.30 proceeds step-by-step through this juncture, which begins in m. 4 and continues through the beginning of m. 6.

As shown in figure 4.30a, Coltrane moves to a pitch on beat 2 that he hasn't emphasized before—the 3rd, E—seemingly implying the end of the first section and signaling the change to the new scale in

Figure 4.29. "Flamenco Sketches," John Coltrane's solo (complete).

the following measure. Figure 4.30b shows Chambers's reaction to this implication: he plays a bass line that strongly implies a move to A♭ in the following measure. At this point, things get interesting. While Chambers's bass line does *eventually* seem to imply a move to A♭, its first part strongly moves to C on beat 4. As shown in figure 4.30c, Coltrane seems to think that Chambers missed the signal to change to the next mode and intends to stay in C major. As a result, in a split-second decision, Coltrane changes course, playing a figure that would allow him to continue improvising in the key of C major. In figure 4.30d, we can see that both musicians have set up strong implications of moving to different keys on the downbeat of m. 5: Coltrane's melody suggests a continuation in C major, Chambers's bass line implies a decisive move to A♭ mixolydian. Figure 4.30e

Figure 4.29. (continued)

shows that Coltrane and Chambers seem to hear the implication of each other's improvisations, and they modify their improvisations to try to arrive on the same key at the same time. Of course, since both musicians change course, they still end up conflicting with each other on the downbeat of m. 5: Chambers jumps to C, while Coltrane jumps to A♭. The musicians eventually sort things out, however, with Chambers moving to A♭ on the downbeat of m. 6.

At the end of the next section, in m. 8, Coltrane seems to want to avoid the problems of the previous change and unambiguously signals the change to the new key. As shown in figure 4.31, Coltrane signals the move to B♭ by repeating the pitch F—the dominant of the subsequent B♭ major scale—and by crescendoing and broadening into the downbeat

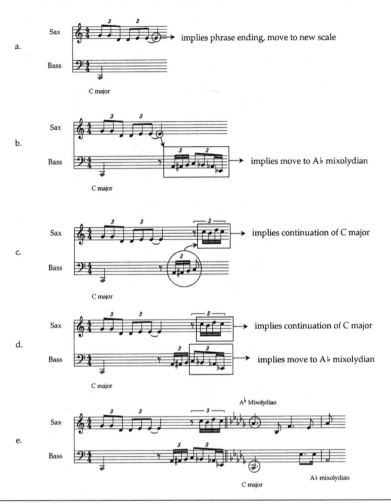

Figure 4.30. "Flamenco Sketches," John Coltrane's solo, mm. 4–6.

Figure 4.31. "Flamenco Sketches," John Coltrane's solo, mm. 8–9.

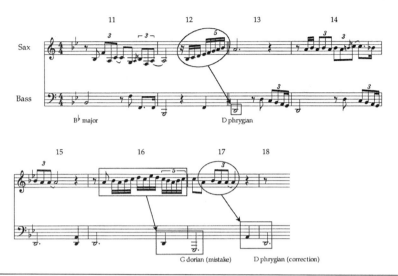

Figure 4.32.   "Flamenco Sketches," John Coltrane's solo, mm. 11–18.

of m. 9. Coltrane also emphasizes the change in a way that cannot be notated in the score: he modulates the timbre of the F, which may have been the result of his visually signaling the change to the new section by, say, raising and lowering his saxophone, which could cause the change in timbre by changing the angle of his mouthpiece and reed.

In the change to the next section, shown in figure 4.32, Chambers again seems unsure where Coltrane is heading. Coltrane finishes his phrase on an A at the end of m. 11, but Chambers seems indecisive about whether to set up the move to D phrygian by playing an A on beat 4, and instead ends up playing an F, as if he were planning on continuing in B♭ major. However, as Coltrane is playing, Chambers seems to decide that Coltrane's strongly forward-moving flurry of notes on beats 3 and 4 is meant to signal a change to the new scale, and instead of moving down a 5th from the F to B♭, moves to D on the downbeat. Four measures later, Chambers hears Coltrane begin another flurry of notes, which he again interprets as a signal to change to the next mode, and, accordingly, moves to G on the downbeat of the next measure. However, when Coltrane continues to emphasize the same pitches—A and B♭—he had emphasized at the beginning of his solo over D phrygian, Chambers realizes that he made the change too soon—that Coltrane intended to stay on D phrygian—and moves back to D at the beginning of the next measure.

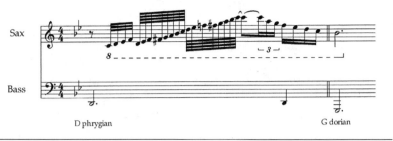

Figure 4.33. "Flamenco Sketches," John Coltrane's solo, mm. 20–21.

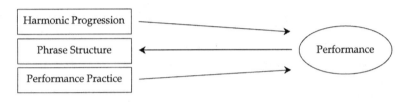

Figure 4.34. Performance schematic, "Flamenco Sketches."

Chambers and Coltrane do synchronize for the change to the final section, transcribed in figure 4.33. Here, Coltrane signals the change with a grand, sweeping melodic gesture that rushes to its high point before relaxing and broadening into B♭ on the downbeat of the next measure. Chambers correctly divines Coltrane's intentions, sets up the move to G dorian by playing its dominant, D, on beat 4, and they arrive together on the same harmony on the downbeat of m. 21.

Reworking the standard-practice schematic diagram to reflect this performance would result in the example given in figure 4.34. Here, the harmonic progression and head arrangement still exert a controlling force over the performance, but the parameter of the phrase structure has been broken down; the length of each section of music is not predetermined, but rather it is negotiated—as we saw, at times more successfully than others—between the musicians in the course of the performance.[20]

Ornette Coleman's "Chronology"

From *The Shape of Jazz to Come* (1959), Ornette Coleman's "Chronology" moves toward free jazz by breaking down the parameter of a predefined harmonic progression.[21] The ensemble on this recording includes Coleman on alto saxophone, trumpeter Don Cherry, bassist Charlie Haden, and drummer Billy Higgins. This ensemble notably omits a

Figure 4.35. "Chronology," phrase structure.

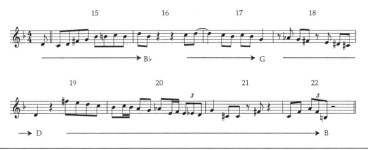

Figure 4.36. "Chronology," Coleman's improvisation over the bridge, mm. 15–22.

common member of the rhythm section, the pianist. Because one of the pianist's primary roles in a jazz ensemble is to play chord voicings that define the harmonic progression of the tune being performed, omitting the pianist allows the other musicians more freedom to improvise without worrying about clashing with an underlying harmony. In the case of "Chronology," it even allows a piece to be composed without any predetermined harmonic progression whatsoever. This is not to say that there is no underlying sense of tonality, however. In the A sections of the composition (the phrase structure is charted in figure 4.35), the melody does convey a strong sense of being in F major.[22] Interestingly, while this composition follows the common AABA formal scheme, there is an unusual difference: the A sections are only seven measures long, rather than the more common eight-measure phrase lengths. In this composition, the B section, or bridge, is left open for improvisation, a common characteristic of AABA tunes composed by jazz musicians; examples of AABA tunes in which the bridge is left open for improvisation include Count Basie's "Lester Leaps In," Charlie Parker's "Anthropology" and "Scrapple from the Apple," Sonny Rollins's "Oleo," and countless others.

Figure 4.36 transcribes Coleman's improvisation over the B section of the head. This improvised melody contrasts with the "composed" melody of the A section in a number of ways. First, in the A section, the melody consists primarily of the notes of the F major scale, with only occasional chromatic embellishments, while the B section improvisation contains a wider variety of pitches. Second, the phrases in the A section further strengthen the feeling of an F tonic by leading to F in m. 4 and to an arpeggiation of an F major triad in m. 7, while Coleman's phrases in the B section lead to several different pitches: B♭ in m. 16, G in m. 17, D in m. 19, and B♮ in m. 22. These melodies also differ in their character or "feel"; the A section feels more static, with the melody zigzagging up and down within a fairly narrow melodic range, while the B section's longer gestures create more of a feeling of forward motion.

Combined with the AABA form, this contrast in character—relatively static A sections versus a relatively forward moving B section—makes this composition feel like the common jazz form known as "rhythm changes." In chapter 2, the deep structure of rhythm changes was, in fact, theorized in very similar terms: the A section was described as the relatively static prolongation of the tonic, while the B section was described as goal-directed motion toward that tonic. What's interesting is that while rhythm changes is usually thought of as, literally, a set of "changes"—that is, a specific chord progression—this performance creates the "feel" of rhythm changes without specifying a progression of chords. Paradoxically, "Chronology" seems to be "rhythm changes" minus the "changes." We will see in the analysis that follows that Coleman and Cherry continue this contrast in "feel" between the A and B sections in their improvisations.

Figure 4.37 transcribes the first chorus of Don Cherry's improvised solo. It is interesting to note that while the composed tune has the unusual feature of seven-measure A sections, the musicians revert to the more common eight-measure phrase lengths for their improvisations.

Several factors contribute to a feeling of stasis in the first and second A sections (mm. 1–8 and 9–16) of Cherry's improvisation. First, his improvised melody is very repetitive, being composed mostly of repeated, monomaniacal A♭s. His melody also is constrained to a fairly narrow tessitura, primarily taking place within the boundaries of the diminished 5th D–A♭; it only briefly dips down into a lower register in mm. 13–14 before returning to cadence on F in m. 15. Cherry also creates stasis by segmenting his improvisation into short phrases that do not flow across structural boundaries; he ends his first A section in m. 7, his second A in m. 15. Bassist Charlie Haden also

Figure 4.37. "Chronology," Don Cherry's solo, mm. 1–32.

contributes to stasis throughout this section by playing a very repetitive bass line that also tends to zigzag around within a fairly narrow range. Even when Haden creates a longer, more expansive gesture, as in mm. 6–9, he slows down the motion with changes in direction and chromatic passing and neighbor notes, taking thirteen beats to ascend the minor 7th from G in m. 6 to F in m. 9.

Cherry's improvisation on the B section (mm. 17–24) contrasts markedly with his first two A sections. Where his A sections felt static, his B section creates a very strong sense of forward motion. In this section, he improvises longer, less segmented gestures that cover a wider range in a shorter time span and make use of a broader pitch spectrum than the previous sections. Beginning in m. 17, he descends through more

Figure 4.37. (continued)

than an octave of an almost-complete chromatic scale before changing direction in m. 19. Within the space of m. 21, he skyrockets through an arpeggiation that takes him from F♯ up an 11th to B♮ before again changing direction. In m. 23, he begins the final phrase of this section, and, significantly, this fast, scalar phrase contributes to the strong forward motion by flowing across the structural boundary and into the final A section in m. 25. By flowing from the B section into the final A section this phrase heightens the similarity in feel between this performance and one based on rhythm changes. Haden also contributes to the sense of forward motion with his bass line throughout this section. Like Cherry, he too covers much more ground in a shorter amount of time, while avoiding the repetitive zigzags of his A sections.

Figure 4.38. "Chronology," Ornette Coleman's solo, mm. 1–32.

In the final A section, mm. 25–32, both Cherry and Haden return to improvisations that sound static in comparison to the forward-moving B section. Cherry again improvises shorter, more segmented gestures made up primarily of a relatively limited pitch collection—this time the pitches of the F major scale—and ends in m. 32, emphasizing the structural boundary between this section and the following A section. Haden also returns to playing a bass line that contains frequent changes of direction within a fairly narrow range, destroying the strong forward motion that he helped create in the B section.

Figure 4.38 transcribes the first chorus of Coleman's improvised solo. Coleman also creates stasis in his improvisation over the A sections, which he contrasts with forward motion in his B section.

Figure 4.38. (continued)

In his first A section, mm. 1–8, Coleman improvises two phrases, one ending in m. 3 and one in m. 7, creating a feeling of segmentation. Likewise, in his second A section, mm. 9–16, he improvises two short phrases separated by rests (mm. 9–10 and mm. 11–12), followed by a longer phrase that ends in m. 16. Like Cherry, Coleman contributes to stasis in these sections by improvising melodies that feel segmented and do not flow across structural boundaries into the following section. Unlike Cherry, however, Coleman does not always differentiate his A sections from his B sections by using contrasting pitch collections. Rather, Coleman creates contrast by improvising melodies that differ in shape and character, not necessarily in pitch content. In his first A section, his melodies often zigzag around, frequently changing

Figure 4.39.   "Chronology," Coleman's solo, mm. 5–7.

direction, creating a feeling of activity, rather than purposeful motion. His second phrase, mm. 5–8, is a good example. In this phrase, as shown in figure 4.39, he creates a compound melodic wedge that expands outward from the minor 3rd D–F to the minor 7th B–A by leaping back and forth between a chromatic descent and ascent: the descending line D–D♭–C–B and the ascending line F–G–G♯–A are interleaved, creating a feeling of gradual registral expansion through the first part of the phrase, which is then negated in the second part of the phrase when everything collapses inward, leaving the phrase to end where it began, on D.

Haden's bass line contributes to the feeling of stasis in these A sections by frequently changing directions, regularly returning to F, repeating certain patterns (especially F–A–G–B♭), and remaining constrained primarily to a one-octave range.

In contrast, Coleman creates a feeling of spinning out a longer melody in his B section, mm. 17–24. Several factors contribute to this feeling. First, while his melodies involve zigzag motion, they neverthe-less convey more of a sense of goal-directedness and forward motion. He begins by playing a phrase that descends a minor 7th, from D to E, over the course of mm. 17 and 18. In m. 19, he begins another descent from D to E, this time extending over a four-measure span, to m. 22. Here, he moves upward to begin another descent, this time from C in m. 23 down a minor 9th to B in m. 24, at which point he quickly shoots upward a 12th to F♯. Another factor contributing to the forward motion created in this section is that the melody seems less segmented than that of the A sections; rather than improvising phrases separated by long rests, Coleman's melody in this section sounds more like a continuous stream leading all the way from the beginning of the section, in m. 17, to the beginning of the final A section in m. 25. Finally, as in Cherry's solo, Haden contributes to this forward motion by playing a bass line that is much more goal-directed; his longer

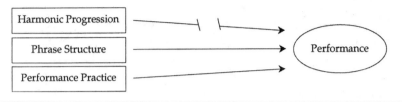

Figure 4.40. Performance schematic, "Chronology."

gestures move more rapidly through a broader musical space than the repetitive, constrained bass lines of the A sections.

In the final A section, Coleman and Haden again create a more static feeling. Coleman's improvisation is very segmented and ends in m. 31, again avoiding flowing across the barline into the next section, while Haden's bass line returns to the character he established in the first two A sections: repetitive, centered on F, and composed primarily of short gestures that frequently change direction.

The relationship between Haden's bass lines and the improvised solos of Cherry and Coleman might be better described as one of *coordination*, rather than interaction. While it's difficult to discern a direct influence between the soloists and bassist—that is, it's hard to look at Haden's bass line and see how his choice of pitches was a reaction to something played by Cherry or Coleman, and vice versa—they do work together to convey a sense of stasis in the A sections and one of motion in the B sections. Reworking the standard-practice jazz paradigm to reflect this performance would result in the example in figure 4.40. Here, the musicians conform to the standard head arrangement and instrumental roles, and coordinate their improvised parts to convey a convincing sense of an AABA rhythm-changes phrase structure. However, the controlling parameter of the predefined harmonic progression has been broken down; the musicians are not constrained to improvising within a set of predetermined changes, but may freely choose pitches to construct melodies as long as those melodies convey the tune's phrase structure.

"Free Jazz" and "Ascension"

While an extensive survey of free jazz is beyond the scope (and aim) of this work, I would like to round out this chapter by briefly discussing and comparing two performances in which the controlling parameters of harmonic progression, phrase structure, and head arrangement have been broken down almost completely. The two pieces—Ornette Coleman's "Free Jazz" and John Coltrane's "Ascension"—are both considered to be important and influential examples of free jazz, and they share some interesting similarities as well as some striking differences.[23] Both performances feature unusual large ensembles in which most of the instruments are doubled. "Free Jazz" is performed by a double quartet consisting of two reed players (Ornette Coleman and Eric Dolphy), two trumpeters (Don Cherry and Freddie Hubbard), two bassists (Scott LaFaro and Charlie Haden), and two drummers (Billy Higgins and Ed Blackwell). Similarly, "Ascension" features two alto saxophonists (Marion Brown and John Tchicai), three tenor saxophonists (John Coltrane, Pharoah Sanders, and Archie Shepp), two trumpeters (Freddie Hubbard and Dewey Johnson), and two bassists (Art Davis and Jimmy Garrison), but only one pianist (McCoy Tyner) and one drummer (Elvin Jones). Both performances also feature a similar large-scale form in which collectively improvised ensemble passages alternate with individual musicians' solos. Because of their density and sonic complexity, these performances are extremely difficult—if not impossible—to transcribe into musical notation and therefore my discussion will refer to specific time points on the recordings themselves.

Even though "Free Jazz" and "Ascension" have much in common, they sound very different. "Free Jazz" has a much drier, more spare sound, in which the musicians weave lines contrapuntally around one another. The trumpets and reeds tend to play with a dry, light tone quality at a medium dynamic level, the bassists tend to play with a relatively light *pizzicato*, and the drummers play with soft, crisp attacks, rarely letting their cymbals ring for long periods of time. The result is that even when all eight of the musicians are playing, there is a clarity to the sound that allows a listener to clearly hear each individual musician's lines. In "Ascension," on the other hand, the musicians create more of a wild "wash" of sound; they play much more aggressively, loudly, and use more sustained tones to create a dense sound "mass" in which it is difficult to pick out individual parts. As a result, the ensemble passages in "Free Jazz" sound like a collection of individual musicians interacting with one another, while those in "Ascension" create more of a feeling of musicians suppressing their individuality and losing themselves in a collective musical act. In addition, "Free Jazz" sounds relatively static in comparison to "Ascension"; it tends to stay within a restricted range of dynamics and intensity, while "Ascension" surges from soft to very loud, from intense to *extremely* intense. In the liner notes to "Ascension," trumpeter Marion Brown describes the energy and intensity of the recording session, saying that it had "that kind of thing in it that makes people scream. The people who were in the studio *were* screaming. I don't know how the engineers kept the screams out of the record."

Another difference between the performances lies in the quality and nature of the interaction and coordination between players. "Free Jazz" places an emphasis on melodic interaction. The musicians have melodic "conversations," a kind of "developing variation" in which the musicians spin out improvised melodic lines based on motives and phrases used by the other musicians. At this point, I would like to lead the reader through a few examples from the first few minutes of the recording of "Free Jazz," describing the ways that musicians interact and coordinate their parts. The piece begins with a short ensemble passage that breaks into two parts of different character. In the first part, which extends from the beginning to 0:05 (that is, to the fifth second of the track), the musicians play fast, fluttery lines, before moving to the second, contrasting part beginning at 0:06. In this section, which extends to 0:21, the musicians play a series of spontaneously created, sustained sonorities. One can hear Coleman in the left channel entering slightly before the rest of the musicians, making it seem that the other musicians chose their pitches in reaction to Coleman's. The first solo, that of bass clarinetist Eric Dolphy, begins at 0:21. I would like to point out two examples of melodic interaction that stand out in the first part of Dolphy's solo. First, at 0:42, one of the trumpet players interjects a repeated descending two-note motive, which Dolphy reacts to immediately, imitating it through 0:45. Another, slightly longer example begins at 1:54. Here, Dolphy begins playing a repeated pitch, to which both trumpet players and Coleman react immediately by playing different repeated pitches. Dolphy follows this at 2:00 with a serpentine, bebop-ish line that winds around within a narrow range, which is immediately picked up and imitated by Coleman and one of the other trumpet players before Dolphy returns to it and continues his improvisation. As the solo continues, this kind of activity increases, with the other musicians more continuously improvising, reacting to Dolphy's motives, as well as interjecting motives that Dolphy responds to. By the end of the solo, the other musicians are improvising so much that the demarcation between Dolphy's solo and the subsequent ensemble passage is blurred. In *Free Jazz*, Jost describes this process of passing motives back and forth between the musicians as one of "motivic chain-associations," which "constantly renews from within the flow of musical ideas."[24] This interactive process is similar to what we saw in the Bill Evans Trio's performance of "Autumn Leaves"—the musicians pass motives back and forth, imitating and responding to one another—except that in this performance the musicians are not constrained by a specific harmonic progression or phrase structure.

While the organizing interactive principles in "Free Jazz" involve a more or less continuous musical conversation between the players, "Ascension" involves less direct musical interaction. Rather, the musicians coordinate their parts to create homogeneous blocks of sound based on specific motives, pitches, and scales. The piece begins with an ensemble section in which John Coltrane introduces a short melodic motive that implies B♭ minor, notated in figure 4.41. The other saxophone and trumpet players all begin improvising around this motive in free time, while the rhythm section creates a sustained sonic backdrop.

By 0:55, the music has gradually morphed into something new, with the musicians all sustaining high pitches. It's hard to determine how the musicians decided to make the change, as no individual musician seemed to lead the way. This passage based on high, sustained pitches continues until 1:18. At this point, John Coltrane again takes the lead, descending rapidly to the lowest register of his horn, which

Figure 4.41.   "Ascension," opening motive.

Figure 4.42. "Ascension," 2:25, F phrygian motive.

the other musicians respond to by playing fast, agitated lines, creating quite a different character from the first part of the ensemble section. This section continues through 1:48, at which point the musicians move into another contrasting section in which they improvise parts that flutter in an agitated manner around a sustained single pitch, a D. Right before all the musicians begin their improvisations around this pitch, it is possible to hear a single player (although it's difficult to tell exactly who it is) introducing a sustained D, to which the others immediately react. The musicians continue to improvise around this pitch, as well as what seems to be the pitches of the D phrygian mode, through 2:25, when one of the trumpet players plays a G♭, then continues with the motive transcribed in figure 4.42, which implies a new modal center of F phrygian. All of the other players again respond immediately and begin basing their improvisation on the F phrygian mode, specifically emphasizing the characteristic semitone G♭–F.

This section continues until approximately 3:50, at which point the ensemble begins to fade out, and John Coltrane gradually moves to the foreground for his solo. As his solo begins, the rhythm section begins to emphasize a key center of B♭ minor, the key in which the performance began.

The strong and immediate response of the musicians to the changes of key center in the opening four minutes of this performance makes it seem likely that these changes were not entirely spontaneous. Rather, one suspects that John Coltrane had provided a simple formal plan for this section, one in which the musicians would move from B♭ minor to D phrygian, then to F phrygian, before returning to the initial key for the first solo.[25] In this respect, this performance is similar to "Flamenco Sketches," which as we saw earlier also involved improvising over a series of scales. The control this plan exerts over this performance seems much weaker than that of "Flamenco Sketches," however. Whereas in "Flamenco Sketches," the goal of the musicians seemed to be to explore the specific harmonic qualities and melodic tendencies of each scale, in "Ascension" the musicians seem to take each scale as a point of departure, playing much more freely over each section. Furthermore, the overriding goal of each musician in "Ascension" seems to be to contribute to the total sonic texture in which the whole ensemble sound is more important than any one individual part.

The solo sections in "Ascension" also differ from those of "Free Jazz." As we saw in "Free Jazz," the soloist and the other musicians are engaged in musical conversations, tossing ideas and motives back and forth. In "Ascension," on the other hand, each soloist improvises over a rhythmic and harmonic backdrop provided by the rhythm section, and the other saxophonists and trumpet players don't play at all until the following ensemble section. As a result, each solo sounds more individual; rather than building a solo by interacting with the other horn players, the soloist is freer to develop the improvisation as he wishes, with interaction taking place primarily between the soloist and the rhythm section. While the interaction between the musicians during the solo sections of "Free Jazz" tended to involve motivic development, in "Ascension" the soloist and rhythm section interact and coordinate their parts to create varying levels of intensity and musical climaxes. I would now like to consider John Coltrane's solo on "Ascension" and discuss the ways that he and the members of the rhythm section coordinate and interact throughout the improvisation.

Coltrane's solo begins at around 3:50. Over the course of his solo, Coltrane creates an overall crescendo and increase in activity and intensity that peaks at around 6:07, at which point all of the other musicians enter and begin the next collectively improvised ensemble passage. Figure 4.43 graphically charts the levels of intensity created by Coltrane and the rhythm section throughout this solo,[26] and I am using the term *intensity* to refer both to quantitative and to qualitative characteristics of the music.

Quantitatively, Coltrane and the rhythm section members create surges in intensity by increasing the levels of various musical parameters, including dynamics, tempo, rhythmic activity, register, harmonic density, tone quality, and so forth. In this performance, the musicians use these technical means to serve a musical purpose, which is to create a qualitative increase in dynamic energy and tension that

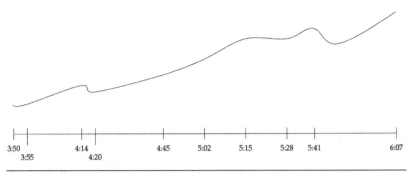

3:50   4:14   4:45   5:02   5:15   5:28 5:41   6:07
   3:55   4:20

Figure 4.43. "Ascension," John Coltrane's solo, graph of intensity level.

builds throughout the solo, creating a continual "ascension" to higher and higher levels of expressive intensity.

At 3:50, the rhythm section locks in, with each member fulfilling their standard roles: bassist Jimmy Garrison plays a walking bass line, pianist McCoy Tyner comps, and drummer Elvin Jones begins playing regular time-keeping patterns. At 3:55, Coltrane begins playing very rhythmically, repeating a three-note pattern, and the members of the rhythm section (especially Jones) respond by increasing their activity, resulting in a gradual heightening of intensity and dynamic level. This increase continues through 4:14, when Coltrane stops playing the rhythmic, three-note pattern, and begins playing more melodically. The rhythm section responds by pulling back, returning to simpler, less active playing, which results in a slight drop in intensity. Beginning at 4:20, Coltrane begins playing shorter phrases in a more and more agitated manner, which the rhythm section again responds to by increasing their rhythmic activity, resulting in a gradual increase of intensity that extends through 4:45. At this point, Coltrane reaches a high, screeching note, and the rhythm section again responds: Tyner and Jones lock up their parts, playing the same rhythm, further increasing the intensity. This increase in intensity created by the rhythm section spurs Coltrane on to even further heights, and both Coltrane and the rhythm section continue to increase their dynamic levels and intensity through 5:02. At this point, Tyner and Jones again lock up their rhythms, cranking the intensity up yet another notch. At approximately 5:15, the level of intensity reaches its highest point so far, and the musicians respond accordingly: Coltrane plays high, squealing notes, Jones plays fast and furious rhythms on his tom-toms, and Garrison abandons his walking bass line and begins playing sustained *arco* tones.

This high point continues through 5:28, at which point the rhythm section pulls back, again reverting to simpler, less active playing, causing a slight drop in intensity and dynamic level. Almost immediately, however, they again begin to build to another climax. All of the musicians contribute to this increase in intensity: Coltrane's lines become shorter and more agitated, Tyner accelerates his rhythms and moves his voicings higher and higher up the keyboard, Jones again increases his rhythmic activity, and Garrison's bass line gradually ascends to a higher range. They peak at 5:41, and after a slight dip in intensity again begin building toward a new high point, which arrives at 6:07. At this point, all of the other musicians enter, beginning the next ensemble section.

Unlike the restrained, relatively static feel created in "Free Jazz," "Ascension" feels wild, dynamic, and intense. We see in Coltrane's solo that he and members of the rhythm section all work together to build to higher and higher levels of intensity, seemingly without limit. Again, while "Free Jazz" and "Ascension" share some common organizing principles—both involve large ensembles improvising with only limited constraining factors—they sound and feel very different, as a result of the way the musicians coordinate and interact with one another. In "Free Jazz," the musicians carry on melodic conversations within a static framework, whereas in "Ascension," the musicians coordinate and interact to create surges in dynamic level and intensity.

Coda

The goal throughout this work has been to explore the ways that interaction between musicians can affect each individual musician's improvisation. We saw in the first three chapters that in standard-practice jazz this interaction takes place within a set of constraints, including performance practices such as the head arrangement and standard instrumental roles, as well as the harmonic progression and phrase structure of the tune being improvised upon. In the performances examined in this chapter, these constraints are gradually, then almost completely, broken down, resulting in a need for heightened interaction between the players. We saw that this interaction can take place in a number of ways: the musicians can interact melodically, passing motives back and forth, as in "Autumn Leaves" and "Free Jazz"; the musicians can interact to negotiate a composition's formal boundaries, as in "Flamenco Sketches"; the musicians can coordinate their parts to convey a sense of phrase structure, as in "Chronology"; and the musicians can interact and coordinate to create dramatic, dynamic climaxes, as in "Ascension."

As I have attempted to show, I think that an analysis of an individual musician's improvisation that fails to consider the simultaneously improvised parts of the other members of a small jazz group is missing something essential. While it is true that many improvised solos can be very interesting to examine in and of themselves, one can gain a fuller picture of the improvisational process and a greater understanding of how a jazz performance works as a whole by examining not only the structure of an individual improvisation but also the complex network of interaction and communication taking place between the players. Furthermore, certain improvisations *need* to be studied in context: Miles Davis's choice of colorful pitches, for example, can only be heard as colorful when considered in relation to the accompaniment provided by the piano and bass; likewise, Bill Evans's improvised gestures on "Autumn Leaves" are as influenced by motives in Scott LaFaro's simultaneous improvisation as by the harmonic progression and voice-leading of the tune. I feel that in moving beyond a focus on the single improvised line to a consideration of the entire texture of a jazz performance, an analyst can come closer to capturing and understanding the dynamic fluidity of jazz improvisation.

Endnotes

Chapter 1

1. For an overview of this topic and the controversies surrounding it, see Kay Kaufman Shelemay, ed., *Musical Transcription*, Garland Library of Readings in Ethnomusicology, Vol. 4 (New York: Garland, 1990). All of the transcriptions in this work are my own.

2. Cannonball Adderley and Milt Jackson, *Things Are Getting Better* (1958), Fantasy/Original Jazz Classics OJCCD-032-2 (1991). A few quick definitions: A "tune" consists of a melody and its accompanying harmony. A "jazz standard" is a tune well known among jazz musicians (and aficionados) and forms part of their basic repertoire. A "chorus" consists of one complete cycle through the harmonic progression associated with a "tune." In the case of "Groovin' High," the tune is thirty-two measures long, which means that each improvised chorus will also be thirty-two measures long.

3. The touchstone for a lot of recent theorizing about signification in jazz is Henry Louis Gates, *The Signifying Monkey* (New York: Oxford University Press, 1989). See, for instance, Robert Walser, "Out of Notes," in *Jazz Among the Discourses*, ed. Krin Gabbard, 165–188 (Durham, NC: Duke University Press, 1995). Reading Adderley's switch from bebop to blues in terms of signifying, one could argue that by making the switch, Adderley articulates a historical consciousness in which he musically acknowledges a genealogical relationship between the more "modern," urban style of bebop and its roots in the rural tradition of the blues.

4. Steve Larson, "Schenkerian Analysis of Modern Jazz" (PhD diss., University of Michigan, 1987); and "Schenkerian Analysis of Modern Jazz: Questions About Method," *Music Theory Spectrum* 20, no. 2 (1998): 209–241.

5. Evans discusses and demonstrates this in his recorded interview with Marian McPartland on *Marian McPartland's Piano Jazz*, The Jazz Alliance TJA 12004 (1978).

6. Steven Block, "Pitch Class Transformation in Free Jazz," *Music Theory Spectrum* 12, no. 2 (1990): 181–200. Block's analysis reproduced in figure 1.8 is Copyright 1990, University of California Press. Reproduced with permission.

7. John Coltrane, *Ascension* (1965), Impulse MVCI-23016 (1991).

8. The labels Block uses to describe the trichords and tetrachords in this example refer to Allen Forte's well-known list of pitch-class sets: the first integer in each hyphenated label specifies the number of distinct pitch classes (or cardinality of) the set; the other integer designates the position of the set within the list of all possible sets of that cardinality,

where the sets are ordered according to interval class content. See Allen Forte, *The Structure of Atonal Music* (New Haven, CT: Yale University Press, 1973), 179–181.

9. *Ascension* will in fact be the subject of further discussion in chapter 4.

10. Ed Sarath, "A New Look at Improvisation," *Journal of Music Theory* 40, no. 1 (1996): 1–38.

11. Charles Keil, "Motion and Feeling through Music," *The Journal of Aesthetics and Art Criticism* 24, no. 3 (1966): 337–349. Keil's "Table of Contrasts," Example 1.9, Copyright 1966, Blackwell Publishing. Reproduced with permission.

12. Leonard Meyer, *Emotion and Meaning in Music* (Chicago: University of Chicago Press, 1956).

13. Keil, "Motion and Feeling through Music," 337–338.

14. Jean-Jacques Nattiez, *Music and Discourse: Toward a Semiology of Music*, trans. Carolyn Abbate (Princeton, NJ: Princeton University Press, 1990).

15. Miles Davis, *Kind of Blue* (1959), Columbia/Legacy CK 64935 (1997).

16. William Thomson, "On Miles and the Modes," *College Music Symposium* 38 (1998), 17–32.

17. For more on phenomenology and music analysis, see David Lewin, "Music Theory, Phenomenology, and Modes of Perception," *Music Perception* 3, no. 4 (1986): 327–392.

18. Paul Rinzler, "Preliminary Thoughts on Analyzing Musical Inter-action Among Jazz Performers" *Annual Review of Jazz Studies* 4 (1988): 153–160. Rinzler's notion of "accenting the end of formal units" will be examined more closely in chapter 3.

19. Paul Berliner, *Thinking in Jazz: The Infinite Art of Improvisation* (Chicago: University of Chicago Press, 1994). Aspects of Berliner's work will be discussed more thoroughly in chapter 3.

20. Ingrid Monson, *Saying Something: Jazz Improvisation and Interaction* (Chicago: University of Chicago Press, 1996).

21. This commonly occurs in what is known as a "jam session," where any number of musicians "sit in," or perform, with a "house" rhythm section without prior rehearsal.

22. Charlie Parker, "Now's the Time," *Original Bird: The Best of Bird on Savoy* (1945), Savoy Jazz ZDS 1208 (1988).

23. Although Dizzy Gillespie is primarily (and famously) known as a trumpeter, this recording demonstrates that he was also a proficient pianist.

24. I have used various means to represent the important features of each tune that I talk about without including the melody (which is the part of a composition specifically protected under copyright). In figure 1.19 I have included only the opening motive of the melody and then its rhythm. In later examples, I will compose "surrogate" tunes that will take the place of the compositions that I wish to discuss. The reader can find complete copies of these melodies in various fake books.

25. Chapter 3 further defines and explores head arrangements, and chapter 4 will examine performances that break down this standard practice.

26. The twelve-bar blues is one of the most common types of compositions in jazz. It consists of three four-measure phrases harmonized with one of several possible harmonic progressions. Chapters 2 and 3 will more fully explore the harmony and form of the twelve-bar blues.

27. As a general rule, the difference in length between the long and short notes is indirectly proportional to the tempo; that is, at a faster tempo, the eighths are more even, and at a slower tempo the difference may be more exaggerated. Common practice in jazz dictates that this pattern be written as two eighth notes, with the understanding that they are to be played unevenly.

28. Even though the backbeat is not on the strong beats 1 and 3, jazz musicians expect the hi-hat to play on 2 and 4, and therefore it functionally defines the strong and weak beats of the meter. When musicians get lost in performance and want to figure out where they are, they will often listen first to the bass and ride pattern to get the beat, and then listen to the hi-hat to figure out where they are in the measure.

29. The word "comping" is usually explained as deriving from the verb "to ac*comp*any," but some musicians say it comes from the verb "to *comp*lement."

30. Keil borrows the term "vital drive" from André Hodeir, who briefly describes it, saying: "There is another element in swing that resists analysis and that I would hesitate to mention if my personal impressions had not been echoed by many jazz musicians. What is involved is a combination of undefined forces that creates a kind of 'rhythmic fluidity' without which the music's swing is markedly attenuated." André Hodeir, *Jazz: Its Evolution and Essence* (New York: Grove, 1956), 207; quoted in Keil, "Motion and Feeling through Music," 341.

31. For an example of Williams's drumming, see Miles Davis, *The Complete Concert 1964* (1964), Columbia/Legacy C2K 48821 (1992).

32. "Blues by Five" (Red Garland), from *Cookin' with the Miles Davis Quintet* (1956), Prestige OJCCD-128-2 (1987). This performance will be examined more closely in chapter 3.

33. The Cannonball Adderley Quintet, *In San Francisco* (1959), Riverside OJCCD-035-2 (1991).

34. Because this transcription is focusing on the nonregular rhythmic aspects of the rhythm section, the drummer's regular rhythmic patterns (the ride pattern and backbeat) have not been transcribed. Nevertheless, Hayes does continue these patterns through this section.

Chapter 2

1. Charlie Parker, "Now's the Time" (1945), from *Original Bird, the Best of Bird on Savoy*, Savoy Jazz ZDS 1208 (1989).

2. For a more detailed discussion of the principles of piano voicing, see Mark Levine, *The Jazz Piano Book* (Petaluma, CA: Sher Music, 1989).

3. George Russell, *The Lydian Chromatic Concept of Tonal Organization* (New York: Concept Publishing, 1959).

4. For examples of jazz pedagogy texts based on a chord/scale approach, see Mark Levine, *The Jazz Theory Book* (Petaluma, CA: Sher Music, 1995), and Scott Reeves, *Creative Jazz Improvisation* (Englewood Cliffs, NJ: Prentice Hall, 1995).

5. This terminology in fact derives from the mainstream of nineteenth-century harmonic theory: "change" is a direct translation of "Wechsel," a common technical designation in (for instance) the harmonic theories of Hugo Riemann. See his *Harmony Simplified, or the Theory of the Tonal Functions of Chords*, trans. Rev. Henry Bewerunge (London: Augener & Co., 1895).

6. It should be noted that not all jazz musicians play from lead sheets; many learn compositions by ear or by rote. Using a lead sheet simply allows us to notate a composition's melody and harmonic progression for discussion and analysis.

7. *The Real Book* is an illegal but ubiquitous fake book, with no author, editor, or publisher given.

8. José Bowen raises similar issues in his exploration of various recordings and printed versions of Thelonious Monk's composition "Round Midnight." See José Bowen, "The History of Remembered Innovation: Tradition and Its Role in the Relationship between Musical Works and Their Performances," *The Journal of Musicology* 11, no. 2 (Spring 1993): 139–173.

9. Traditionally, the word "function" is used to refer to chordal identity: that is, in the key of F, the tonic is F^{Maj}, the subdominant below is Bb^{Maj}, and the dominant above is C^{Maj}. In this work, I'm using "function" to refer to relations *between* harmonies, and not to the harmonies them-selves. My use of the word in this sense is based on the work of David Lewin, although my functions are somewhat less rigorously defined. See David Lewin, "A Formal Theory of Generalized Tonal Functions," *Journal of Music Theory* 26, no. 1 (1982): 23–60; and *Generalized Musical Intervals and Transformations* (New Haven, CT: Yale University Press, 1987).

10. My use of "chaining" and "nesting" derives from Edward R. Pearsall's "Trees and Schemas: A Cognitive Approach to Music Analysis" (PhD diss., University of Wisconsin–Madison, 1993), 97–103. While Pearsall uses these concepts to discuss the construction and perception of melodic schema, I have transposed them to the harmonic domain.

11. Technically, this interval is a diminished 5th, whereas the literal mean-ing of the term "tritone"—the interval created between two pitches that are three whole steps apart—refers to an augmented 4th. However, jazz musicians use this term informally to designate any six-semitone

interval, whether a diminished 5th or an augmented 4th, a usage I, too, will follow.

12. Fétis, describing the diatonic augmented 4th and diminished 5th, says that "these intervals define modern tonality by means of the energetic tendencies of their constituent sounds: the leading-note tending toward the Tonic, and the fourth degree towards the Third." He goes on to say that "this character, which is eminently tonal, cannot constitute a state of dissonance; in reality the augmented Fourth and diminished Fifth are employed as consonances in various harmonic successions." Although he defines them as consonances, he describes them as a special kind of consonance, which he calls "appelative," because of their unique "energetic tendencies" toward resolution. François-Joseph Fétis, *Traité complet de la théorie et de la pratique de l'harmonie*, 11th ed. (Paris: Brandus et Cie., 1875), 8–9. Translated in Matthew Shirlaw, *The Theory of Harmony* (London: H. W. Gray, 1917), 341–342.

13. In the abstract, there is no way to predict the goal of the forward motion created by the streams of harmonies in figure 2.15; these progressions could begin and end on any one of the harmonies. When used in actual musical settings, however, additional parameters, such as meter, phrase structure, voice-leading, melodic shape, or an overall sense of key allow a certain harmony to be identified as the goal of the progression, and the other harmonies can be heard as progressing toward that goal. We will see examples of the chaining of both dominant and tritone-substitution functions later in the chapter in the analysis of "Rhythm-A-Ning," and in both cases these chains are heard as progressing toward a specific goal.

14. Henry Martin theorizes the tritone substitution in a similar way in "Jazz: A Syntactical Background," *Annual Review of Jazz Studies* 4 (1988): 9–30. He says that "the dominant seventh and the tritone substitution function alike because of their common tritone, the critical interval of resolution in the dominant-tonic progression." He goes on to describe the relationship in set-theoretic terms, explaining that the M7 function—that is, multiplication by 7 mod 12—maps a dominant seventh harmony onto its tritone substitution. Although this transformation works for the examples he gives—he successfully maps $E\flat^7$ onto A^7 with this function—it doesn't work for all harmonies. Specifically, it doesn't work with harmonies that are based on even-numbered pitch classes. In his example, he converts the root, 3rd, and 7th of $E\flat^7$ into the pitch-class set [3, 7, 1]. Multiplying each element of this set by 7 mod 12 results in pitch-class set [9, 1, 7], which contains the root, 3rd, and 7th of A^7. Applying this same transformation to the root, 3rd, and 7th of C^7, or [0, 4, 10], does not map these pitches onto its tritone substitution, $F\sharp^7$, but instead preserves its identity: $0 * 7 = 0; 4 * 7 = 4$ mod 12; $10 * 7 = 10$ mod 12.

15. This kind of harmonic ambiguity is not unique to jazz, of course. In Act 3 of *Tristan and Isolde*, Wagner uses these exact harmonies to affect a modulation from F minor to B major by reinterpreting a $C7^{(\flat5)}$ (the altered dominant of F) as $F\sharp^{7(\flat5)}$ (the altered dominant of B). For a thorough

discussion and analysis of this passage see Brian Hyer, "Tonal Intuitions in *Tristan and Isolde*" (PhD diss., Yale University, 1989), 349–352.

16. Noam Chomsky, *Cartesian Linguistics* (New York: Harper & Row, 1966), 32–33.

17. For a more extended introduction to generative grammar, see Janet Fodor, *Semantics: Theories of Meaning in Generative Grammar* (New York: Crowell, 1977).

18. Alan M. Perlman and Daniel Greenblatt, "Miles Davis Meets Noam Chomsky: Some Observations on Jazz Improvisation and Language Structure," in *The Sign in Music and Literature*, ed. Wendy Steiner (Austin: University of Texas Press, 1981), 169–183.

19. Thelonious Monk, *Criss Cross* (1963), Columbia/Legacy CK 48823 (1993).

Chapter 3

1. Thomas Owens, "Form," in *The New Grove Dictionary of Jazz*, ed. Barry Kernfeld (New York: St. Martin's Press, 1994), 396–400.

2. Charlie Parker, "Now's the Time" (1945), from *Original Bird, The Best of Bird on Savoy*, Savoy Jazz ZDS 1208 (1988).

3. Barry Kernfeld, *What to Listen for in Jazz* (New Haven, CT: Yale University Press, 1995), 40.

4. I was not able to obtain permission to reproduce some tunes. For these I will use newly composed "surrogate" compositions. These surrogates will have similar-sounding names, and will retain all of the structural features (harmonic progression, phrase structure, rhythmic patterns, etc.) of the tunes.

5. Kernfeld, *What to Listen for in Jazz*, 41.

6. Clifford Brown and Max Roach, "Cherokee," from *Study in Brown* (1955), EmArcy 814 646-2 (1990).

7. Miles Davis, "Blues by Five," from *Relaxin' with the Miles Davis Quintet* (1956), Prestige OJCCD-190-2 (1991).

8. In deference to copyright provisions, the melodies for "Rhythm-A-Ning" and "How High the Moon" are not included in these examples.

9. Thelonious Monk, "Rhythm-A-Ning," from *Criss Cross* (1963), Columbia/Legacy 48823 (1993).

10. Thelonious Monk, "Misterioso" (1947), from *The Best of the Blue Note Years*, Blue Note B2-95636 (1991).

11. Calling this formal anomaly a "mistake" is, of course, speculative; it's entirely possible—but, I think, quite unlikely—that Monk decided to insert an extra measure into this improvised chorus. In the many blues compositions recorded by Monk, this is the only one I know of in which he adds an extra measure to a standard twelve-bar blues chorus. There does exist an additional recorded performance of "Misterioso" which is from the same session as the one I discuss. In this alternate take, there

are no formal irregularities; Monk takes only a single twelve-measure chorus before returning to the head.

12. Rinzler, "Analyzing Interaction Among Jazz Performers," 157.
13. Berliner, *Thinking in Jazz,* 319.
14. Miles Davis, "Blues by Five" (Red Garland), from *Cookin' with the Miles Davis Quintet* (1956), Prestige OJCCD-128-2 (1987).
15. Miles Davis, "E.S.P.," *E.S.P.* (1965), Columbia CK46863 (1991).
16. Because this example is primarily concerned with the use of rhythm to define structural boundaries, the transcription only supplies the rhythm of the piano and bass parts, not the actual pitches.

Chapter 4

1. Mark Gridley, *Concise Guide to Jazz,* 4th ed. (Upper Saddle River, NJ: Prentice Hall, 2004), 144.
2. James Lincoln Collier, *The Making of Jazz: A Comprehensive History* (New York: Delta, 1978), 454.
3. David Such, *Avant-garde Jazz Musicians: Performing "Out There"* (Iowa City: University of Iowa Press, 1993), 4.
4. Frank Tirro, *Jazz: A History* (New York: W. W. Norton, 1993), 372.
5. Bill Evans Trio, *Portrait in Jazz* (1959), Riverside OJCCD-088-2 (1992).
6. The reader is encouraged to consult *The New Real Book*, Vol. 1 (Petaluma, CA: Sher Music, 1988) for a complete lead sheet for this composition.
7. The voice-leading of inner voices suggested by the tune will be examined later.
8. Of course, at the beginning of a performance, listeners would not have any frame of reference that would allow them to hear the initial C^{-7} harmony as a IV chord in G minor. This discussion, however, is focusing on the performer's perspective, and the performer could think of it as such from the start.
9. For a thorough discussion of this approach, see Mark Levine's *The Jazz Theory Book.*
10. Thomas Owens, "Charlie Parker: Techniques of Improvisation" (PhD diss., University of California at Los Angeles, 1974).
11. Gunther Schuller, "Sonny Rollins and the Challenge of Thematic Improvisation," in *Musings: The Musical World of Gunther Schuller* (New York: Oxford University Press, 1986), 86–97.
12. The "blues" scale comprises a minor pentatonic scale with one additional pitch, the diminished 5th. A "blues" scale built on G would consist of the tonic (G), the minor 3rd (B♭), the perfect 4th (C), the diminished 5th (D♭), the perfect 5th (D), and the minor 7th (F).
13. Miles Davis, *Kind of Blue* (1959), Columbia/Legacy CK 64935 (1997).
14. Nat Hentoff, "An Afternoon with Miles Davis," *Jazz Review* 2 (December 1958): 11–12.

15. George Russell, *The Lydian Chromatic Concept of Tonal Organization* (Cambridge, MA: Concept Publishing, 1959).

16. Barry Kernfeld, "Adderley, Coltrane and Davis at the Twilight of Bebop: The Search for Melodic Coherence" (PhD diss., Cornell University, 1981).

17. William Thomson, "On Miles and the Modes."

18. Hentoff, "An Afternoon with Miles Davis," 12.

19. Ekkehard Jost, *Free Jazz* (New York: Da Capo Press, 1994), 22.

20. An alternate take for "Flamenco Sketches" does exist, and is included in the re-mastered version of *Kind of Blue*. The alternate version features different improvised solos and, in general, a lower level of interaction between the rhythm section and the soloists. Nevertheless —as was the case in the master take—the changes from one mode to the next tend to be smoother in Miles Davis's solo than in John Coltrane's.

21. Ornette Coleman, *The Shape of Jazz to Come* (1959), Atlantic 1317-2 (1987).

22. The melody is not notated for copyright reasons.

23. Ornette Coleman, *Free Jazz* (1960), Atlantic 1364-2 (1992); John Coltrane, *Ascension* (1965), Impulse MVCI-23016 (1991). My analysis focuses on Edition I.

24. Jost, *Free Jazz*, 59–60.

25. In *John Coltrane: His Life and Music*, Lewis Porter discusses the issue of Coltrane's formal plan for *Ascension*, saying: "Bob Thiele handed out lead sheets at the session. It's uncertain what he gave out. . . . Alice Coltrane reconstructed some descending chords for the published version, but its not obvious how to relate those to the recording." Later he writes: "Several commentators have noticed that 'Ascension' seems to be loosely based on scales"—an interpretation that corresponds to my own hearing of this passage. See Lewis Porter, *John Coltrane: His Life and Music* (Ann Arbor: University of Michigan Press, 1998), 263.

26. This graphing of levels of intensity is influenced by the work of Ingrid Monson. See Monson, *Saying Something*, 138–139.

Recordings Cited

Following is a list of recorded jazz performances examined in this work. The list is organized by chapter, with the performances listed in the order that they are discussed.

Chapter 1

"Groovin' High" (Dizzy Gillespie), from Cannonball Adderley and Milt Jackson, *Things Are Getting Better* (1958), Fantasy/Original Jazz Classics OJCCD-032-2 (1991). Personnel: Cannonball Adderley (alto saxophone), Milt Jackson (vibes), Wynton Kelly (piano), Percy Heath (bass), Art Blakey (drums).

"Ascension" (John Coltrane), from John Coltrane, *Ascension* (1965), Impulse MCVI-23106 (1991). Personnel: John Coltrane, Pharoah Sanders, Archie Shepp (tenor saxophone), Marion Brown, John Tchicai (alto saxophone), Freddy Hubbard, Dewey Johnson (trumpet), McCoy Tyner (piano), Art Davis, Jimmy Garrison (bass), Elvin Jones (drums).

"So What" (Miles Davis), from Miles Davis, *Kind of Blue* (1959), Columbia/Legacy CK 64935 (1997). Personnel: Miles Davis (trumpet), John Coltrane (tenor saxophone), Cannonball Adderley (alto saxophone), Bill Evans (piano), Paul Chambers (bass), Jimmy Cobb (drums).

"Now's the Time" (Charlie Parker), from Charlie Parker, *Original Bird: The Best of Bird on Savoy* (1945), Savoy Jazz ZDS 1208 (1988). Personnel: Charlie Parker (alto saxophone), Miles Davis (trumpet), Dizzy Gillespie (piano), Curley Russell (bass), Max Roach (drums).

Miles Davis, *The Complete Concert 1964* (1964), Columbia/Legacy C2K 48821 (1992). Personnel: Miles Davis (trumpet), George Coleman (tenor saxophone), Herbie Hancock (piano), Ron Carter (bass), Tony Williams (drums).

"Blues by Five" (Red Garland), from *Cookin' with the Miles Davis Quintet* (1956), Prestige OJCCD-128-2 (1987). Personnel: Miles Davis (trumpet), John Coltrane (tenor saxophone), Red Garland (piano), Paul Chambers (bass), Philly Joe Jones (drums).

"Spontaneous Combustion" (Cannonball Adderley), from The Cannonball Adderley Quintet, *In San Francisco* (1958), Riverside OJCCD-035-2 (1991). Personnel: Cannonball Adderley (alto saxophone), Nat Adderley (cornet), Bobby Timmons (piano), Sam Jones (bass), Louis Hayes (drums).

Chapter 2

"Now's the Time" (Charlie Parker), from Charlie Parker, *Original Bird: The Best of Bird on Savoy* (1945), Savoy Jazz ZDS 1208 (1988). Personnel: Charlie Parker (alto saxophone), Miles Davis (trumpet), Dizzy Gillespie (piano), Curley Russell (bass), Max Roach (drums).

"Rhythm-A-Ning" (Thelonious Monk), from Thelonious Monk, *Criss Cross* (1963), Columbia/Legacy CK 48823 (1993). Personnel: Thelonious Monk (piano), Charlie Rouse (tenor saxophone), John Ore (bass), Frankie Dunlop (drums).

Chapter 3

"Now's the Time" (Charlie Parker), from Charlie Parker, *Original Bird: The Best of Bird on Savoy* (1945), Savoy Jazz ZDS 1208 (1988). Personnel: Charlie Parker (alto saxophone), Miles Davis (trumpet), Dizzy Gillespie (piano), Curley Russell (bass), Max Roach (drums).

"Cherokee" (Ray Noble), from Clifford Brown and Max Roach, *Study in Brown* (1955), EmArcy 814 646-2 (1990). Personnel: Clifford Brown (trumpet), Harold Land (tenor saxophone), Richie Powell (piano), George Morrow (bass), Max Roach (drums).

"Rhythm-A-Ning" (Thelonious Monk), from Thelonious Monk, *Criss Cross* (1963), Columbia/Legacy CK 48823 (1993). Personnel: Thelonious Monk (piano), Charlie Rouse (tenor saxophone), John Ore (bass), Frankie Dunlop (drums).

"Misterioso" (1947), (Thelonious Monk) from *Thelonious Monk: The Best of the Blue Note Years*, Blue Note B2-95636 (1991). Personnel: Thelonious Monk (piano), Milt Jackson (vibes), John Simmons (bass), Max Roach (drums).

"Blues by Five" (Red Garland), from *Cookin' with the Miles Davis Quintet* (1956), Prestige OJCCD-128-2 (1987). Personnel: Miles Davis (trumpet), John Coltrane (tenor saxophone), Red Garland (piano), Paul Chambers (bass), Philly Joe Jones (drums).

"E.S.P." (Wayne Shorter), from Miles Davis, *E.S.P.* (1965), Columbia CK46863 (1991). Personnel: Miles Davis (trumpet), Wayne Shorter (tenor saxophone), Herbie Hancock (piano), Ron Carter (bass), Tony Williams (drums).

Chapter 4

"Autumn Leaves" (Joseph Kosma), from Bill Evans Trio, *Portrait in Jazz* (1959), Riverside OJCCD-088-2 (1992). Personnel: Bill Evans (piano), Scott LaFaro (bass), Paul Motian (drums).

"Flamenco Sketches" (Miles Davis), from Miles Davis, *Kind of Blue* (1959), Columbia/Legacy CK 64935 (1997). Personnel: Miles Davis (trumpet), John Coltrane (tenor saxophone), Cannonball Adderley (alto saxophone), Bill Evans (piano), Paul Chambers (bass), Jimmy Cobb (drums).

"Chronology" (Ornette Coleman), from Ornette Coleman, *The Shape of Jazz to Come* (1959), Atlantic 1317-2 (1987). Personnel: Ornette Coleman (alto saxophone), Don Cherry (trumpet), Charlie Haden (bass), Billy Higgins (drums).

"Free Jazz," from Ornette Coleman, *Free Jazz* (1960), Atlantic 1364-2 (1992). Personnel: Ornette Coleman (alto saxophone), Eric Dolphy (alto saxophone, bass clarinet, and flute), Don Cherry and Freddie Hubbard (trumpet), Charlie Haden and Scott LaFaro (bass), Billy Higgins and Ed Blackwell (drums).

"Ascension" (John Coltrane), from John Coltrane, *Ascension* (1965), Impulse MCVI-23106 (1991). Personnel: John Coltrane, Pharoah Sanders, Archie Shepp (tenor saxophone), Marion Brown, John Tchicai (alto saxophone), Freddie Hubbard, Dewey Johnson (trumpet), McCoy Tyner (piano), Art Davis, Jimmy Garrison (bass).

Bibliography

Berliner, Paul. *Thinking in Jazz: The Infinite Art of Improvisation*. Chicago: University of Chicago Press, 1994.

Block, Steven. "Pitch Class Transformation in Free Jazz." *Music Theory Spectrum* 12, no. 2 (1990): 181–200.

Bowen, José. "The History of Remembered Innovation: Tradition and Its Role in the Relationship between Musical Works and Their Performances." *The Journal of Musicology* 11, no. 2 (Spring 1993): 139-173.

Chomsky, Noam. *Cartesian Linguistics*. New York: Harper & Row, 1966.

Collier, James Lincoln. *The Making of Jazz: A Comprehensive History*. New York: Delta, 1978.

Fétis, François-Joseph. *Traité complet de la théorie et de la pratique de l'harmonie*. 11th ed. Paris: Brandus et Cie., 1875.

Fodor, Janet. *Semantics: Theories of Meaning in Generative Grammar*. New York: Crowell, 1977.

Forte, Allen. *The Structure of Atonal Music*. New Haven, CT: Yale University Press, 1973.

Gates, Henry Louis. *The Signifying Monkey*. New York: Oxford University Press, 1989.

Gridley, Mark. *Concise Guide to Jazz*. 4th ed. Upper Saddle River, NJ: Prentice Hall, 2004.

Hentoff, Nat. "An Afternoon with Miles Davis." *Jazz Review* 2 (December 1958): 11–12.

Hodeir, André. *Jazz: Its Evolution and Essence*. New York: Grove, 1956.

Hyer, Brian. "Tonal Intuitions in *Tristan and Isolde*." PhD diss., Yale University, 1989.

Jost, Ekkehard. *Free Jazz*. New York: Da Capo Press, 1994.

Keil, Charles. "Motion and Feeling through Music." In *Music Grooves*, 53–76. Chicago: University of Chicago Press, 1994.

Kernfeld, Barry. "Adderley, Coltrane and Davis at the Twilight of Bebop: The Search for Melodic Coherence." PhD diss., Cornell University, 1981.

_____. *What to Listen for in Jazz*. New Haven, CT: Yale University Press, 1995.

Larson, Steve. "Schenkerian Analysis of Modern Jazz." PhD diss., University of Michigan, 1987.

Levine, Mark. *The Jazz Piano Book*. Petaluma, CA: Sher Music, 1989.

_____. *The Jazz Theory Book*. Petaluma, CA: Sher Music, 1995.

Lewin, David. "A Formal Theory of Generalized Tonal Functions." *Journal of Music Theory* 26, no. 1 (1982): 23–60.

_____. "Music Theory, Phenomenology, and Modes of Perception." *Music Perception* 3, no. 4 (1986): 327–392.

_____. *Generalized Musical Intervals and Transformations*. New Haven, CT: Yale University Press, 1987.

Martin, Henry. "Jazz: A Syntactical Background." *Annual Review of Jazz Studies* 4 (1988): 9–30.

Meyer, Leonard. *Emotion and Meaning in Music.* Chicago: University of Chicago Press, 1956.

Monson, Ingrid. *Saying Something: Jazz Improvisation and Interaction.* Chicago: University of Chicago Press, 1996.

Nattiez, Jean-Jacques. *Music and Discourse: Toward a Semiology of Music.* Translated by Carolyn Abbate. Princeton, NJ: Princeton University Press, 1990.

Owens, Thomas. "Charlie Parker: Techniques of Improvisation." PhD diss., University of California at Los Angeles, 1974.

————. "Form." In *The New Grove Dictionary of Jazz,* edited by Barry Kernfeld, 396–400. New York: St. Martin's Press, 1994.

Pearsall, Edward. "Trees and Schemas: A Cognitive Approach to Music Analysis." PhD diss., University of Wisconsin–Madison, 1993.

Perlman, Alan M., and Daniel Greenblatt. "Miles Davis Meets Noam Chomsky: Some Observations on Jazz Improvisation and Language Structure." In *The Sign in Music and Literature,* edited by Wendy Steiner, 169–183. Austin: University of Texas Press, 1981.

Porter, Lewis. *John Coltrane: His Life and Music.* Ann Arbor: University of Michigan Press, 1998.

Reeves, Scott. *Creative Jazz Improvisation.* Englewood Cliffs, NJ: Prentice Hall, 1995.

Riemann, Hugo. *Harmony Simplified, or the Theory of the Tonal Functions of Chords.* Translated by Rev. Henry Bewerunge. London: Augener & Co., 1895.

Rinzler, Paul. "Preliminary Thoughts on Analyzing Interaction Among Jazz Performers." *Annual Review of Jazz Studies* 4 (1988): 153–160.

Russell, George. *The Lydian Chromatic Concept of Tonal Organization.* Cambridge, MA: Concept Publishing, 1959.

Sarath, Ed. "A New Look at Improvisation." *Journal of Music Theory* 40, no. 1 (1996): 1–38.

Schuller, Gunther. "Sonny Rollins and the Challenge of Thematic Improvisation." In *Musings: The Musical World of Gunther Schuller,* 86–97. New York: Oxford University Press, 1986.

Shelemay, Kay Kaufman, ed. *Musical Transcription.* Garland Library of Readings in Ethnomusicology, Vol. 4. New York: Garland, 1990.

Shirlaw, Matthew. *The Theory of Harmony.* London: H.W. Gray, 1917.

Such, David. *Avant-garde Jazz Musicians: Performing "Out There."* Iowa City: University of Iowa Press, 1993.

Thomson, William. "On Miles and the Modes." *College Music Symposium* 38 (1998): 17–32.

Tirro, Frank. *Jazz: A History.* New York: W. W. Norton, 1993.

Walser, Robert. "Out of Notes." In *Jazz Among the Discources,* edited by Krin Gabbard, 165–188. Durham, NC: Duke University Press, 1995.

Index